AIRCRAFT WRECKS IN THE MOUNTAINS AND DESERTS OF CALIFORNIA

1909-1996

SECOND EDITION

The author, Gary Pat Macha, on the trail looking for a World War ll era military training plane thought to be a Vultee BT-13. (Carl Deeds) Region 7.

Aircraft Wrecks in the Mountains and Deserts of California

1909-1996

Second Edition

Gary Pat Macha

Info Net Publishing
San Clemente, California

Cover design by Vivi Boas
Cover photos and
Frontispiece photo by Gary Pat Macha
Typesetting and book design
by Paul Rahmes - Forza Design

Aircraft Wrecks in the Mountains and Deserts of California.

Published by Info Net Publishing
PO Box 3789 San Clemente, CA 92674
Telephone: (714) 489-9292 Fax: (714) 489-9595
E-mail: infonetpub@aol.com

PRINTED IN CANADA

Library of Congress Cataloging-in-Publication Data

Macha, Gary Pat
Aircraft Wrecks in the Mountains and Deserts of California
Gary Pat Macha -- 2nd ed.
CIP: 96-079070

ISBN: 0-924272-08-2

Dedication

For my son, Patric J. Macha,
a successful wreckfinder in his own right.

1976

1996

CONTENTS

CONTENTS

North American SNJ-2
#2549
US Navy

Crashed in Santa Rosa Mnts. on search mission looking for missing USN Grumman F4F's. Crash date was 2/42. (D. Hammer) Region 1.

Wreck of Vought F4U-1A USMC #17562 that crashed 3/30/44 following mid-air collision. (G.P. Macha) Region 5.

FOREWORD

This book is not intended to be a trail guide to the more than fourteen hundred aircraft crash sites listed herein. However, directions are included to a few special wrecks to serve as model sites, though on balance, I have not included exact wreck site locations by longitude and latitude, or township and range, nor do I advocate the wholesale removal of aircraft wreckage. If you want, however, to locate and visit a specific crash site, I offer the following suggestions.

1. Equipment: Hiking shoes or boots, hat, sunglasses, long pants, windbreaker, pancho, canteens, first aid kit, camera, compass, knife, maps.

2. Physical condition: Know your limitations. Physical fitness is essential. Use the buddy system, don't go after a plane wreck alone.

3. Research: Find out as much as possible about the area that you are going to visit. Be aware of rattlesnakes, ticks, poison oak. Ask about water quality and availability. Understand the terrain, and know how to use a topographic map. In California it is especially important to understand how difficult it can be to hike in chaparral environments. Always obtain permission to enter private land, and appropriate permits in wilderness areas. Obtain land use permits to remove wreckage.

4. Locating the wreck: Fly over the area to be investigated. Drive, walk, hike, or climb into your search area. Look for sunlight reflecting off metal, small pieces of aircraft in dry stream or creek beds, small burned areas, clipped trees or other incongruities in the natural setting.

5. Identifying the wreckage: Photograph the site. Note location on a map. Look for registration numbers, serial numbers, manufacturers ID plate, and note other markings and colors. Is the wreck marked (painted with red or yellow X's), unmarked, burned, scattered, buried, partly or mostly removed? If wreck is unmarked and unsalvaged, look for human remains as California still has a number of unlocated aircraft. Never disturb, tamper with, or remove anything from a crash site that is under investigation. Veteran and vintage crash sites are resources and sometimes monuments. Please leave them as you found them unless you are assisting in a restoration effort. Use caution at old military crash sites where unexploded ordinance and live ammo may still be present. Use common sense and enjoy the search for your goal.

List of Abbreviations Used in this Book

AAB	Army Air Base
AFB	Air Force Base
CAP	Civil Air Patrol
CIA	Central Intelligence Agency
ELT	Emergency Locator Transmitter
FAA	Federal Aviation Administration
LTV	Ling Temco Vought
NAA	North American Aviation
NAS	Naval Air Station
NWC	Naval Weapons Center
NTSB	National Transportation Safety Board
USAAC	United States Army Air Corps
USAAF	United States Army Air Force
USAAS	United States Army Air Service
USAF	United States Air Force
USCG	United States Coast Guard
USFS	United States Forest Service
USMC	United States Marine Corps
USMCAS	United States Marine Corps Air Station
USMCTC	United States Marine Corps Training Center
USN	United States Navy
WASP	Womans Air Service Pilot
WW II	World War II

ACKNOWLEDGMENTS

This book would not have been possible without the cooperation and assistance of the following agencies, newspapers, and individuals: Federal Aviation Administration, National Park Service, National Transportation Safety Board, United States Air Force, United States Forest Service, American Aviation Historical Society, county sheriff departments throughout the State of California, the *Los Angeles Times, Fresno Bee, and San Francisco Chronicle*. Special thanks go to Civil Air Patrol squadrons whose members I've interviewed and flown with for over thirty years.

The following individuals provided stories, photographs, insight, artifacts, guide service, flight time, and encouragement: Raymond Nelson, Maj. C. L. Burrell, Civil Air Patrol, David Hatfield, Lindal and Sewell Griggers, Lawrence Webster, Willard Farhquar, Phil Pister, Bob Buhrle, Mike Alt, Pat Quinn, Scotty MacGregor, Jerry Bond, Ira Chart, Jack Farley Jr., Clark Harvey, Robert Koch, Francis S. Yarnell, Glen H. Sexton, David Chichester, Michael J. McIntyre, Don Mitchell, Jon K. Lawson, Gary Chrisman, Jerry Boal, Jeff Boal, Mary Jane Macha, Patric J. Macha, Charles F. Macha, Chris Macha, Gary Salazar, Joel Levine, Rich Allison, Susan Allison, Donald Lank, Bob Lank, Herb Lank, Jim Rowan, Don Morrison, Tim Stewart, The X-Hunters: Peter Merlin and Tony Moore, Romano Urbat, Dan Hammer, "Wild Bill" Gossett, Tom Gossett, Mike McComb, Chris Spanberg, John Zimmermann, Ben F. Giebeler, Joel Bishop, Gene H. DeRuelle, Elgin F. Gates, Bob Burtness, Ralph Baxter, Rick Flaherty, Nick Veronico, Jack C. West, Don Young, Wayne Bemis, Wyn Selwin, Mark Foster, Roy Wolford, Pat Starkey, Ray Tippo, Brian Gilger, Stan Jones, Chris Killians, William T. Larkins, Wreck Finder Productions (Producer: Carl Deeds, Writer: Harlene Goodrich, Cameraman: Roger Berryderry, and Mike Fortner and Kent Lantz of "Curtiss Wright Historical Association—Project Tomahawk."

Special thanks to my editors Mike Fortner, Linda Chrisman, and Harlene Goodrich.

Scattered wreckage of a Douglas TA-4J USN assigned to VA-124 lies unmarked and scattered in upper Lovelace Canyon N.W. of Big Bear Lake. Wreck dates from 1970. (G.P. Macha) Region 6.

INTRODUCTION

With the growing interest in aircraft recovery and preservation, I have compiled a listing of aircraft that have crashed in the mountains and deserts of California from 1909 to 1996. In the course of my research, I was surprised not only by the number of aircraft wrecks, but that many wreck sites remain virtually undisturbed. It should be understood that I have not visited every site listed herein. Limited time, resources, and the varied geography of California have kept me from many mountain peaks and deep canyons. Poor weather, late summer snowpacks, and the effects of brush and forest fires have thwarted attempts to reach and photograph many crash sites. I will, therefore, welcome additions and corrections to this work.

Man has left an archaeological trail dating back tens of thousands of years. His bones, dwellings, art, and technologies are now part of, or will be part of, the archaeological record. Aircraft archaeology is the study and identification of wrecked or abandoned aircraft. Aircraft archaeology has been a popular pastime in Europe for more than three decades and is now catching on in the United States. While much news has been made regarding recent aircraft finds in the Zuider Zee and the moors of Yorkshire, the American West holds hundreds of equally intriguing relics, many dating from the 1920s and '30s. Aircraft wrecks from the World War II era are now receiving extensive attention as aircraft restorers scramble to obtain parts, fittings, and castings for *F-51s, F6Fs, F4Us*, and a host of other unique aircraft.

The purpose of this work is twofold: to chronicle the approximate location of every aircraft crash site in the mountains and deserts of California, and to provide information on the cause and factors that contributed to these crashes. Unlike freeway automobile accidents that are quickly cleaned up, airplane wrecks that remain for years undisturbed provide us with a sobering opportunity to consider the power of nature and the misjudgments of man. Sadly, the majority of the accidents listed resulted from pilot error, and not from the failure of aircraft systems or structure.

The first aircraft wreck that I visited was a *Douglas C-47B #45-1124 USAF* located at the 11,000-foot level of Mt. San Gorgonio, the highest peak in the San Bernardino Mountains. The *C-47B* had crashed on 11/28/52, and large yellow X's had been painted on the wreck to indicate that this aircraft had been "found," and need not be reported as a "new" wreck. I reached this site in the summer of 1963, before any trails had been cut in this part of the San Gorgonio Wilderness. What lay on the mountainside before me was a recognizable, unburned airplane that had hit the mountain in a blinding snowstorm. Thirteen men died here and their uniforms, parachutes, and other personal effects littered the area. I sat on a large boulder for thirty minutes, stunned by what I saw.

Today a trail passes through the wreckage, now scattered by the movement of successive snowpacks. Hikers have carried much away from the site, and they are sometimes heard to say, "Just an old plane, one of many." For me *#45-1124* is a part of aviation history and a monument to the men who died there.

This book is dedicated to those who lost their lives serving their nation while flying in California. These were brave men and women learning to fly, flying the freight, ferrying aircraft, patrolling our skies, flying rescue missions, or those in transit, like the men aboard *United States Air Force C-47B #45-1124.*

Regional Map

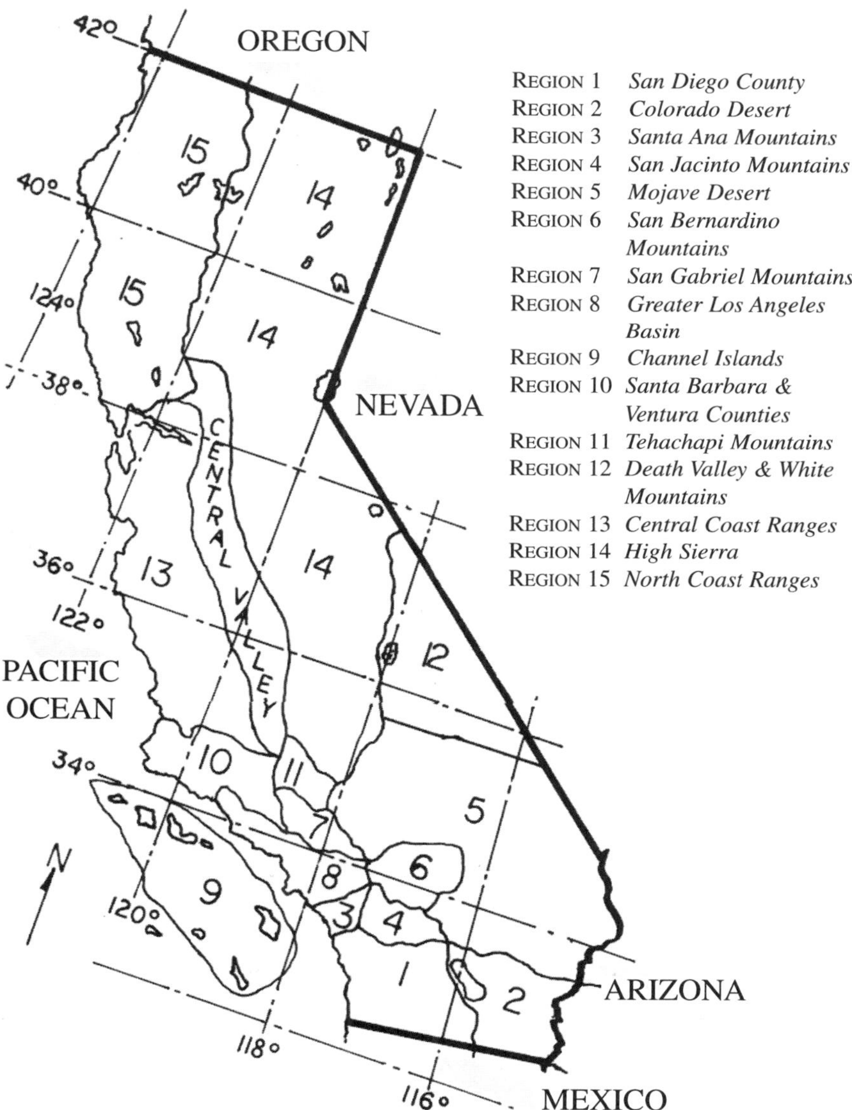

California Regional Reference Map for areas covered in the following chapters.

Aircraft Wrecks in the Mountains and Deserts of California

1909-1996

Second Edition

Grumman F6F-5N USMC. (D. Hammer) Region 6.

US Navy AD-4N. (P.J. Macha) Region 4.

Firebee Drone. (G.P. Macha) Region 9.

Martin B-26 USAAF. (G.P. Macha) Region 6.

1953. Luscombe 8A N1389K. (J. Bishop) Region 12.

Region 1

Region 1 includes the Santa Rosa, Vallecito, Palomar, and Laguna Mountains, as well as all of the coastal hills from the Mexican border north to Oceanside. The eastern boundary of this region is Highway 86 with the Pacific Ocean providing the western limits. The southern boundary is the Mexican border with USMC Camp Joseph Pendleton and Highways 79 and 371 marking the northern limits. The highest point in this area is Toro Peak towering a respectable 8,716 above sea level. More than one hundred wreck sites are located in this region.

12/7/22. *DeHavilland DH-4 US Army Air Service* crashed on the south ridge and east slope of Cuyamaca Mountain in bad weather, killing the pilot and gunner. The engine and some small parts remain along with a memorial plaque designating this site as a state monument. This wreck was not located until 5/12/23 when a cattle rancher happened upon it.

(For further details on 12/7/22 crash please see inset MAP next page)

1925. *Five US Army planes* crashed in the low mountains east of San Diego during a period of bad weather.

1931. *An aircraft of unknown type* crashed in the mountains near the town of Laguna in San Diego County.

1/6/41. *Douglas R2D-1 (DC-2) US Navy* crashed into fog-shrouded Mother Grundy Peak, killing all eleven on board. A few unmarked parts still litter the site.

12/10/41. *Grumman F4F US Navy* lies wrecked and marked in the Superstition Mountains NE of El Centro. This aircraft was part of a flight of six that were bound for San Diego. All were lost. Some were not located until the late 1950s. One hit Laguna Peak. Another crashed at Pine Corners near Julian. Two F4Fs wrecked on the Crawford Ranch and one was found near Warner Springs.

11/3/42. *US Navy aircraft* crashed and burned, killing the pilot while on training flight. Unmarked crash site is near Otay Mountain.

2/1942. *North American SNJ-2 US Navy trainer* #2549 crashed near Rabbit Peak in the Santa Rosa Mountains of Riverside County. Wreck is unmarked and mostly removed. This aircraft had been assigned to the Commander Carrier Division One at North Island Naval Air Station. The crash occurred during search operations for missing 4F4s lost 12/41.

11/30/43. Two *Grumman F6F-3 US Navy aircraft* collided near Barrett Dam in San Diego County. One pilot was killed and one parachuted to safety. Some unmarked parts still visible from aircraft #66161.

Date unknown. *Curtiss C-46 XAGOT, Mexican Civil aircraft*, on mountain south of Dulzura in San Diego County. Wreckage unmarked and scattered.

Date unknown. *Consolidated PBY US Navy* on Tule Mountain in San Diego County. Wreckage marked with yellow **X**'s.

12/7/22. *DeHavilland DH-4 USAAS* wreck site and monument in Cuyamaca State Park, San Diego County, CA. Take State Highway 79 north from Interstate 8 to Green Valley Camp and Picnic Area. Park your vehicle and proceed on foot north of the campground to Monument Trail. Hike two miles on Monument Trail to the junction of West Mesa Fire Road where you will find the Liberty Engine, the wreck monument, and a few small aircraft parts. Best time of year to make this hike is October through May. Mountain Lions are common in this area, so don't go alone!

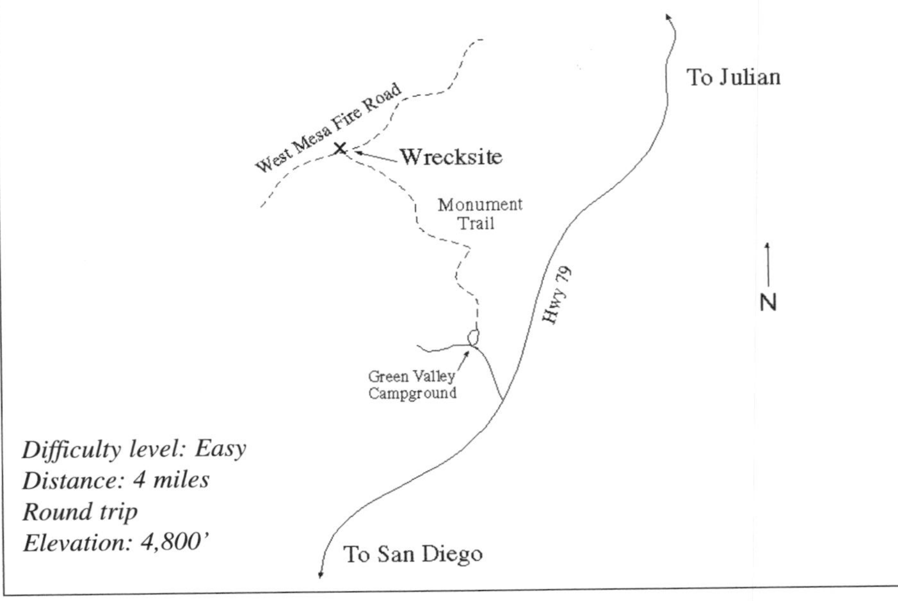

Difficulty level: Easy
Distance: 4 miles
Round trip
Elevation: 4,800'

Region 1

Date unknown. *Lockheed P-38L #44-26695 USAAF* crashed north of the town of Laguna in San Diego County. Scattered wreckage is still visible.

Date unknown. *Chance Vought F4U-1D #57325US Navy* in mountains of San Diego County twenty miles north of Jacumba. Wreck is scattered.

5/30/44. *Consolidated B-24* crashed as the result of a mid-air collision on Mt. Palomar. Twelve men perished in the crash. Scattered wreckage is unmarked and visible.

12/15/44. Two *Grumman TBF USMC aircraft* based at El Toro Marine Air Station collided while on training mission near Lake Hodges, killing all eight men on board. Crash sites are in rugged hills SE of Escondido. Status of wrecks today is unknown.

Date unknown. *Vought F4U-4 #81140 USN* crashed and burned NE of Chula Vista near community of Sunnyside. No other data available.

3/3/46. *Douglas DC-3 American Airlines NC-21799* crashed in bad weather on Tierra Blanca Mountain at the 4,500' level, killing all 28 persons on board. Unmarked parts remain at site.

12/24/46. *Douglas DC-3 Western Airlines NC-45395* crashed on Cuyapaipe Mountain in San Diego County, killing all twelve persons on board. This accident occurred during a period of stormy weather. Marked parts remain visible at the site today. This aircraft was originally delivered to the USAAC as C-47D #42-68715.

Date unknown. *Beechcraft C-45 NC-68228* lies scattered in the mountains near Jacumba in San Diego County.

Date unknown. *Beechcraft SNB #125142 USN* crashed in the mountains near Dulzura in San Diego County. This wreck is still visible and the words NAS. San Diego are on the vertical stabilizer.

Date unknown. A *Taylorcraft lightplane* wreck dating from the early 1950s lies in the hills north of Morena Reservoir in San Diego County. Wreck is overgrown and difficult to see.

Date unknown. *Vought F4U USMC.* is reported to have crashed near or on Mt. San Onofre in northern San Diego County. Status of wreck is unknown today.

Date unknown. *Cessna UC-78 NC-44000* crashed near Lake Hodges in San

Diego County. The wreck has been removed from this site. No other data.

Date unknown. *Vought F4U* listed as unmarked and scattered in the Carrizo Badlands NE of Highway S-2.

Date unknown. *Lockheed F-80 or T-33A USAF* is visible, scattered, and unmarked NW or trailer park near Agua Caliente Springs Airfield.

Date unknown. *North American F-51D USAF* is reported unmarked and scattered in mountains near Lake Henshaw.

1951. *Vought F4U-4 USMC* five miles SW of town of Murietta in the Squaw Mountain Region. Pilot died in crash.

4/18/52. A *Douglas AD-2 attack aircraft* crashed on Mt. San Onofre, killing the pilot. Wreck is mostly removed.

Date unknown. *Lockheed F-80A #44-85208 USAF* crashed east of Toro Peak in the Santa Rosa Mountains of Riverside County, killing the pilot. This wreckage is visible and scattered.

1/28/55. A *US Navy Grumman F9F-5* crashed and burned in bad weather ten miles east of Warner Hot Springs. The pilot was killed in the crash. Wreck is bulldozed over.

Date unknown. *Cessna 140 N89249* crashed near Laguna Junction in San Diego County. Wreck is reported removed.

2/7/57. A *USMC Sikorsky HR2S-1* hit a 2,408' mountain north of Coyote Wells in San Diego County. One crewman suffered minor injuries in the crash. Wreck is removed.

12/19/57. A *Boeing B-47 USAF* based at March Air Force Base crashed on Mt. Palomar during bad weather. All three crewmen were killed in the crash. Wreck is removed.

5/16/59. Two persons died in the crash of an *Aeronca 7DC* at Deer Flat in the Santa Rosa Mountains of Riverside County. Pilot error was listed as the official cause of this accident.

Date unknown. *Sikorsky HRS-2 #129047 USMC* lies wrecked near Case Springs on Camp J.H. Pendleton in upper DeLuz Canyon. Wreck is marked.

12/10/59. *Douglas A-4B #142845 USN* crashed and burned during training flight NE of El Centro in Superstition Mountains. Wreck is unmarked.

1/26/60. *Cessna 180 N7877A* crashed on Mt. Woodson about four miles SW of Ramona in bad weather, killing one person and seriously injuring another.

1960. A *Douglas AD-5N #132525* US Navy hit east of Toro Peak in the Santa Rosa Mountains in Riverside County. Aircraft was assigned to VC-35 at North Island Naval Air Station, is blue, highly visible and unmarked.

8/3/60. *Chance Vought F8U-1 #145405 US Navy* crashed west of Toro Peak on a routine training flight. The pilot was killed and the scattered wreckage of this plane is still visible today.

10/6/60. Two persons were killed and two others were injured when their lightplane crashed on Mt. Palomar during bad weather. Wreck is removed.

1/9/61. A *Douglas A-4C USN* crashed west of Brawley in the US Navy bombing and gunnery ranges that includes the Superstition Mountains. No other data available.

Date unknown. *Chance Vought F80-2 USN #146977* is reported scattered and marked west of Superstition Hills in Borrego Valley.

Date unknown. *Douglas A-4B USN #142845* is burned and marked on the bombing range in the Superstition Mountains of Imperial County.

3/27/61. *North American FJ-4 #39291 US Navy* crashed south of Dulzura at the 2,500' level, killing the pilot. Wreck is mostly removed.

8/24/61. *North American FJ-4 US Navy* crashed in the mountains south of Barrett in San Diego County. Some scattered wreckage is still visible.

9/20/61. *Chance Vought F8U-1 US Navy* crashed on the north slope of Toro Peak in the Santa Rosa Mountains of Riverside County. Wreck is widely scattered.

1/1/62. A *Cessna 172 N7374A* crashed at the 5,500' level of Toro Peak in the Santa Rosa Mountains. All three persons on board survived and were rescued after sustaining only minor injuries in this accident.

7/27/62. *Porterfield N25543* crashed near Warner Springs. This wreck has been completely removed from site. No other data is available on this crash.

8/15/62. *Chance Vought F8U-1 #143728 US Navy* crashed on the east slope of Toro Peak during a routine training flight. This wreckage is marked and visible.

9/17/62. *Mooney Mk 20 N8150E* in hills north of Santee. No other data.

12/23/62. *Piper Cherokee N5652W* crashed and burned two miles east of Julian in bad weather, killing all three persons on board.

10/20/63. *Cessna OE-2 #140088 USMC* crashed NE of Julian on this date. Status of wreck is not known.

2/26/64. *Mace M-101 N352L* crashed three miles north of Brown Field on Otay Mesa, killing the pilot. Wreck is removed.

3/22/64. A *Ryan Navion N91451* crashed in the rugged Agua Tibia Mountains while on a Civil Air Patrol search mission. All three men on board were killed. This accident occurred in bad weather. Wreck is visible and is marked.

4/7/64. *Globe Swift GC1B N2371B* crashed on the west slope of Mt. Laguna, at the 5,700' level, killing the two persons on board. Weather was a factor in this crash.

9/18/65. *Cessna 150 N5807E* crashed in cloudy conditions SW of Thermal in the Santa Rosa Mountains. Wreck is upside down and unmarked.

2/10/66. *Piper Comanche N6829P* crashed in bad weather near Santee at the 3,500' level, killing both persons on board.

4/25/66. *Cessna 150 N8044S* crashed near Julian, killing one person and seriously injuring another.

Date unknown. *Cessna* wreckage reported marked in mountains of Cuyamaca State Park west of Highway 2.

2/4/67. *Porterfield 75C N32315* hit Mt. Laguna in bad weather, killing both persons on board.

4/6/67. *Piper Cherokee N8126W* crashed at the 4,000' level of Mt. Palomar during cloudy weather, killing the pilot. Status of wreck is unknown.

9/5/67. *Bellanca 17-30* crashed on a mountain near San Marcos in cloudy weather, killing both persons on board. This wreck has been removed.

11/19/67. *Piper Cherokee N6556P* crashed in mountains near Warner Hot Springs, killing two persons on board.

5/1/68. *USMC helicopter* crashed on the south slope of Toro Peak, killing one and injuring fifteen. This wreck has been completely removed.

11/2/68. *LTV F-8 USMC* crashed one mile east of Julian in bad weather, killing the pilot. Wreck is removed.

12/21/68. *Ryan Navion, N010H* hit Tecate Peak at the 3,800' level while on a Civil Air Patrol search mission. All three men on board were killed. Scattered wreckage is visible.

12/24/68. *Piper PA-28 N1753J* is located north of Interstate 8 in the In-Ko-Pah Mountains. Status unknown.

4/28/69. *Lightplane* type unknown is wrecked in the Yuha Basin south of Interstate 8.

Patric J. Macha and fuselage section of Fokker F-10A on Shay Mountain. Crash date was 2/23/30. (G.P. Macha) Region 6.

11/22/69. *McDonnell Douglas F-4 US Navy and a USMC LTV F-8* collided over the mountains east of Warner Springs. One crewman died and two parachuted to safety. The scattered wreckage of this mid-air accident is still visible today.

12/24/69. *Cessna 182 N4262Z* hit at the 3,000' level of El Cajon Mountain, killing the only person on board. Fire totally consumed this aircraft, which crashed during a winter storm.

2/28/70. *Aeronca Champion N9895* crashed at the 2,800' level of Otay Mountain, killing the pilot. Poor weather contributed to the cause of this accident.

5/3/70. A *USMC Sikorsky CH-53* crashed at the 6,500' level on the south side of Santa Rosa Peak, killing one and injuring four.

Date unknown. *Aero Commander 600 N1716S* crashed SE of Ocotillo Wells in low hills.

6/12/70. *LTV F-8 USMC* crashed near Ocotillo Wells, killing the pilot. Wreck is mostly removed.

11/30/70. *Piper Cherokee* crashed in the hills near Caliente. The accident occurred during a period of bad weather and both persons on board were killed.

2/19/71. *Piper Apache N7378P* hit San Miguel Mountain in bad weather, killing two persons. Wreck is brown, white, and scattered.

3/28/71. *Cessna 172* crashed in mountains near Warner Springs airfield, killing all four persons on board.

4/23/71. *McDonnell F-4B US Navy* is scattered and unmarked SW of Lake Henshaw in San Diego County.

6/5/71. *Piper Tri-Pacer N48872* crashed and burned six miles north of Escondido, killing the pilot. Very poor weather was listed as a factor in this accident.

2/14/72. *McDonnell Douglas F-4 US Navy* assigned to the Blue Angels flight demonstration team crashed in the Superstition Mountains, killing the pilot. Scattered wreckage remains at site.

7/15/72. Three persons survived the crash of a *lightplane* in the mountains near Ramona.

9/3/72. *Sailplane* hit mountain peak near Mexican border, killing the pilot. Wreck is removed.

9/9/72. *Piper Tri-Pacer N9731D* hit Lyons Peak, killing three persons on board. Status of wreck is not known.

3/8/73. *Three McDonnell Douglas F-4s US Navy* assigned to the Blue Angels crashed in the Superstition Mountains while on a training flight. All three pilots escaped injury. Scattered wreckage is visible.

3/21/73. Four persons perished in the crash of a *lightplane* thirty-five miles NE of Julian.

3/25/73. Two persons survived the crash of their *lightplane* forty miles east of San Diego near Interstate 8.

9/23/73. A *lightplane* with four people on board hit Chiquita Peak at the 4,100' level in cloudy weather. All on board were killed. Weather was listed as a factor in this crash.

11/15/73. *Piper Aztec* crashed near Lawson Valley thirty miles east of San Diego, killing the three people on board. Weather was listed as a factor in this accident.

6/2/74. An *Aero Commander 580* crashed and burned near Santee, killing both people on board. Heavy coastal clouds were a factor in this crash.

5/29/75. One man survived the crash of his *lightplane* at the 1,700' level of Mt. Whitney near Escondido. Coastal clouds were a factor in this accident.

11/6/75. Two persons were killed when their l*ightplane* hit Volcan Mountain near Julian. Poor weather was a factor.

11/17/75. A *Piper Cherokee* hit Cowles Mountain in bad weather, killing both persons on board.

11/19/76. *Cessna 182 N7877A* crashed ten miles east of Palomar in bad weather, killing two persons on board. Wreck is unmarked.

4/1/77. *Rockwell International T-39D US Navy* crashed in Blair Valley, seven miles east of Julian, in the Laguna Mountains. All five aircrew on board were killed. Wreck is removed.

7/1/77. One man was killed when his *sailplane* crashed on Split S Mountain near Ocotillo Wells. Wreck is removed.

12/27/77. *Cessna 182 N3979D* hit Rock Mountain, thirty miles NE of San Diego, killing two persons and seriously injuring a third. Bad weather was a factor in this accident.

4/20/78. A *Beechcraft Duchess N176LD* crashed in the mountains NE of San Diego, killing two persons on board. Site is near Mt. Woodson.

12/1/78. *Piper Tri-Pacer N6034V* lies wrecked near Cuyamaca Peak. Status unknown.

12/5/78. A *Cessna 172* hit Cuyaiape Mountain in bad weather, killing the only person on board.

2/25/79. *Cessna 150* crashed, seriously injuring two persons when they hit Rabbit Peak SW of Thermal.

Liberty engine from DeHavilland DH-4 USAAS at Cuyamaca State Park Monument site. (G.P. Macha) See inset map page 2, Region 1.

8/79. *North American F-51D N33Z* crashed in the Anza Borrego Desert State Park, killing the pilot. The aircraft is said to have broken up in flight. Only a few parts remain.

2/15/80. A *Cessna 421 N15E* crashed four miles SE of Lake Wohlford in bad weather, killing the pilot. Wreck is removed.

3/22/81. *Luscombe Model 8* crashed eight miles SE of Ocotillo Wells, killing the pilot. Weather was a factor in this accident.

1/5/82. *Ryan Navion N4520K* hit Mt. Woodson in San Diego County. All on board died in this weather-related accident.

1/20/82. *Cessna 182* crashed eighteen miles east of Palomar Airport, killing all three people on board. Weather was a primary factor in this accident.

2/8/82. A *Cessna 172 N7737R* crashed in rugged mountains north of Santa Ysabel, killing the pilot. Due to bad weather the wreck was not located until 2/12/82. Wreck is unmarked.

2/22/82. *McDonnell Douglas A-4 USN* is scattered in Superstition Hills SW of Highway 86.

6/1/82. Wreck of *Stinson 108 N97911* is scattered, unmarked, SE of Julian.

11/29/82. *Cessna 150 N67707* in mountains south of Julian. No other data.

12/24/82. Four persons died in the crash of a *lightplane* near Julian. Weather was a factor in this crash.

2/23/83. One person died in the crash of his *lightplane* near Descanso in bad weather.

3/21/83. A *Cessna 170B* crashed in bad weather 1/4 mile east of the Mt. Palomar Observatory, killing both persons on board. Weather was a factor in this crash. Parts remain at site.

9/3/83. *Boeing Vertol CH-46E*, USMC crashed near Case Springs on Camp Pendleton, killing all four crewmen on board. Wreck is removed.

11/10/83. *LTV A-7 US Navy* is scattered on West Mesa of East Fish Creek Mountains.

8/4/84. Two persons were seriously injured in the crash of a *lightplane* near Julian. Pilot error is listed as the cause of this crash.

1/21/85. A *Cessna 185* crashed near Pine Valley, killing two persons. Weather was a factor in this crash.

4/21/85. One person was killed when his *lightplane* hit power lines during bad weather near Rainbow in San Diego County.

6/4/85. *Lightplane* crashed in Coyote Mountains north of Ocotillo. Wreck is unmarked.

7/31/85. *Rockwell International OV-10 USMC* crashed on Mt. San Onofre, killing both crewmen. Wreck is removed.

10/85. *Piper Cherokee* crashed in bad weather near the town of Crest in San Diego County. The pilot was killed in the accident.

1/1/86. Four persons died in the crash of a *lightplane* near El Cajon. Weather was a factor in this crash.

5/10/87. *Chance Vought F4U* crashed and burned seven miles east of Brown Field near Otay Lakes. Two persons died in the crash which occurred while stunts were being performed. Wreck is removed.

4/4/88. *Cessna 150.* One man survived the crash of his lightplane on Guatay Peak about fifty miles east of San Diego. The pilot was eventually rescued by helicopter after trying to walk out from the crash site.

5/7/88. Two persons died when their *Piper Cherokee* crashed into a low mountain at Rancho Cuyamaca State Park.

1988. Eight men were killed in the crash of a *Bell UH-1H* flown by the California National Guard while on a drug interdiction mission at night. The crash site is located in the Jacumba Mountains east of Mountain Spring, near Interstate 8. Wreck is removed.

2/13/89. A *Piper Comanche* crashed on Volcan Mountain NE of Julian, killing both persons on board. Bad weather was a factor in this crash. Status of wreckage is not known.

Date unknown. *McDonnell Douglas F-4 US Navy* reported scattered north of Mexican border near Tecate.

9/18/89. *Lightplane* enroute from San Diego to John Wayne Airport crashed on a hillside near Escondido, killing both men on board. Weather at time of accident was rainy and the pilot may have become disoriented. Wreck is removed.

11/9/89. *Cessna 182RG N2257T* crashed on Otay Mesa east of San Diego, killing two persons and seriously injuring two others. Accident occurred at night. Wreck is removed.

2/18/90. *Cessna 182 N1510U* crashed in mountains near the south end of Lake Henshaw in San Diego County. Both persons on board survived this weather-related accident and were rescued thanks to the efforts of the Civil Air Patrol. Wreck is on Loma Madera Ranch and it will be removed.

6/11/90. *Pitts Special N29MC* in mountains west of Salton Sea Beach. Status unknown.

1/22/94. *Christian Eagle* crashed and burned in hills near Ramona. Wreck is removed.

12/14/94. *Grumman American A4-1* crashed while observing wrecked Cessna 150 N5807E lost on 9/18/65. Both pilot and passenger survived, but were injuried..

12/23/96. *Experimental Home-built Aircraft* crashed in the mountains of San Diego County on the east side of Volcan Mountain. The plane had been enroute from Bullhead City, Arizona to San Diego when it crashed in bad weather killing both men on board.

Cameraman Roger Berry Derry sits in the back seat of a Vultee BT-13 NC62556 near Palm View Peak. (G.P. Macha) Region 4.

Author, Gary Pat Macha, at the site of a Y1B-17 crash. (G.P. Macha) See inset map page 30, Region 4.

REGION 2

Region 2 includes both the Colorado Desert and a portion of the Mojave Desert, as well as numerous mountain systems such as the Orocopia, Chocolate, Chuckwalla, and Cargo Muchacho Mountains. The highest peak in this area is 4,505' Black Butte, which is located in the Chuckwalla Mountains.

The boundaries of Region 2 are Interstate 10 in the north, the Colorado River in the east, the Mexican Border on the south, and Highway 86 in the west. This area is characterized by barren mountains, sand dunes, expanses of flat desert, and the Salton Sea. Only about twenty crash sites are found in this region.

Date unknown. *Vought F4U US Navy* reported in Algodones Dunes south of Glamis.

1940s. *North American B-25 USAAF* is still visible in the Sand Hills south of Highway 78. This wreck is marked and is often reported by pilots flying over the area, but was reported removed in early 1990s.

Date unknown. *Chance Vought F4U US Navy* crashed in Chocolate Mountains. Wreck is marked and visible, about 45 miles SW of Blithe. This F4U disappeared during WWII and was not located until 10/15/47.

Date unknown. *North American F-51 USAAF* crashed north of Highway 78 in Chocolate Mountains. Wreck is unmarked and scattered.

1944. *Consolidated B-24 USAAF* is unmarked and scattered in the Palo Verde Mountains. Visitors to this site reported seeing some machine guns and live ammo in 1972.

Date Unknown. A *Goodyear FG-1 (F4U)* is marked and visible in the northern Chocolate Mountains of Riverside County. Site is NE of Bombay Beach within the bombing and gunnery range.

1950s. *North American FJ-3 #135814 US Navy* is located in the Chuckwalla Mountains NW of Augustine Pass. Pilot is thought to have died in this crash. Wreck is unmarked and scattered.

Date unknown. *Grumman F9F US Navy* scattered on desert near El Centro.
1955. Stinson wreckage is located in Chocolate Mountains and is not marked.

2/17/60. *Chance Vought F8U-1 #145205 US Navy* crashed in the Chocolate Mountains north of Highway 78 and is covered over.

12/18/62. *Cessna 182 N30387T* hit a 1,400' peak twenty miles north of Yuma, Arizona. The wreck lies just inside the California border at the 1,000' level. All three persons on board were killed. Weather was a factor in crash.

Date unknown. *Douglas A-4 USN* scattered in Algodones Dunes south of Highway 78.

North American FJ-3 #135814 US Navy.

Located in the Chuckwalla Mountains. Wreck is unmarked and scattered NW of Augustine Pass. Accident date is late 1950's. (USAF) Region 2.

9/3/64. *LTV F-8E #150881 US Navy* crashed near Lion Head Mountain in Chocolate Mountains. This wreck is scattered and unmarked.

11/17/65. A *US Navy McDonnell F-4B* crashed in Cargo Muchacho Mountains, killing one crewman and slightly injuring another. Wreck is scattered and unmarked.

8/67. *Sikorsky CH-53A #154875 USMC* crashed in Chocolate Mountains. Wreck is unmarked and scattered.

Date unknown. *McDonnell Douglas F-4B US Navy* crashed north of Highway 78 in Chocolate Mountains.

2/18/73. A *Cessna 150 N19116* crashed north of Highway 78 in Chocolate Mountains. This wreck is yellow and white but unmarked.

11/5/73. *McDonnell Douglas F-4J US Navy* crashed in the Chocolate Mountains. Both crewmen were killed in this accident.

4/10/77. *Hiller 12E N90645* crashed near Thermal, killing the pilot. This wreck was not discovered until October, 1977, in spite of an extensive search. Wreck is removed.

4/19/77. A *Grumman F-14 US Navy* crashed in the Chocolate Mountains. Both crewmen safely ejected from the stricken aircraft.

10/2/78. *McDonnell Douglas AV-8A USMC* crashed in Chocolate Mountains, killing the pilot.

11/30/78. *McDonnell Douglas A-4M USMC* crashed in Chocolate Mountains. The pilot safely ejected just before impact.

12/13/84. *Cessna 172 N7301K* crashed in Chuckwalla Mountains in bad weather, killing all three persons on board.

10/28/87. Two *LTV A-7Es of the US Navy* collided over the Chocolate Mountains. Both pilots safely ejected following the collision. Wreckage is scattered and unmarked.

1/23/90. (2) *McDonnell Douglas FA-18 US Navy of the Blue Angels* flight demonstration team collided over the Superstition Mountains. Only one aircraft crashed and the pilot ejected safely. Status of wreck is not known.

2/3/90. *McDonnell Douglas AV-8B USMC* crashed in the Chocolate Mountains while on a routine training mission. The pilot ejected safely and was rescued. Wreck is scattered.

Date unknown. *Piper PA-32 N3206W* scattered south Interstate 8, SE of Holtville.

7/29/90. *Bell UH-1N USMC* crashed in the Chocolate Mountains while on a night training mission. Two men died and three others were injured. Status of wreckage is not known.

3/1/96. A *McDonnell Douglas AV-8B* crashed in the Chocolate Mountains following malfunction and successful pilot bailout. Wreck is unmarked.

Empennage of Douglas C-47 USAF Reserve that crashed in rugged Hagador Canyon 12/14/61 killing the three man crew. (G.P. Macha) Region 3.

REGION 3

Region 3 includes the Santa Ana Mountains, Sheep Hills, and San Joaquin Hills. The highest peak in this area is 5,687' Santiago Peak, also known as Saddleback Mountain. Much of the area is chaparral and grasslands. Region 3 is bordered on the west by the Pacific Ocean, on the north by the 91 and 55 Freeways, on the south by Camp Joseph H. Pendleton, and on the east by Interstate 15. More than sixty crash sites lie within this area.

11/12/42. A *Military aircraft* crashed and burned in Williams Canyon near a mountain community of Silverado. Pilot died in crash. No other data is available. Wreckage is presumed removed.

2/14/43. *Lockheed P-38F #41-2336 USAAF,* flown by flight officer E. L. Smith, crashed on Dawson Canyon on Monument Peak south of Lake Matthews following mid-air collision. Site was visible and marked for many years, but was mostly removed in the 1980s. The pilot made a successful bailout and the second aircraft *AP-38E #41-2072* flown by 2nd Lt. Joseph A. Dolan, returned safely to March Field.

1943. *Douglas SBD USMC* crashed in Lucas Canyon, south of Highway 74, killing both crewman. Wreck is marked and visible today.

1944. *Fairchild GK-1 US Navy* crashed in upper Silverado Canyon. This unmarked wreck is overgrown by chaparral.

1944. *Douglas SBD-5 #29029 USMC* crashed and burned in Aliso Canyon, killing the pilot. This site is located in the Sheep Hills SE of Laguna Beach.

6/22/44. *Douglas SBD-6 #54741 USMC* crashed in the coastal San Joaquin Hills. Wreck is removed.

6/23/44. A *North American F-51D USAAF* crashed near Laguna Canyon following pilot bailout. This site is burned and unmarked.

1944-45. *Grumman FM-1 #15843 USMC* crashed in upper Fremont Canyon in bad weather. The pilot died and the aircraft did not burn. Several attempts have been made to locate this wreck without success. Wreck may have been removed from Jean's Ranch area in mid-1980s by aircraft restorers.

Date unknown. *Military trainer* intact SW of Santiago Peak at Yeager Mesa. Removed in the 1960s.

Date unknown. *Vought F4U-1A USMC* crashed and burned on Irvine Ranch land south of Santiago Reservoir in low hills. Wreckage is scattered and unmarked.

10/14/44. *Curtiss SB2C USMC* crashed in Trabuco Canyon following aileron separation. Both crewmen died in this accident. Status of wreck is unknown.

Date unknown. *Republic P-47D "Razorback" USAAF* crashed in rugged Hagador Canyon, killing the pilot. The engine, armor plate, and other parts remain in a poison oak-covered landscape 200 yards south of USAF C-47 wreck. Wreck was apparently salvaged for metal value in the early 1960s.

1948-49. *Grumman F6F-5N #588287 USMC* lies wrecked at the 3,300' level west of Pleasants Peak. Site is situated on steep slope and is partly burned and unmarked.

Date unknown. *Grumman F7F USMC* crashed in bad weather at Los Pinos

Wreck of Cessna 172 N2619L that hit Modjeska Peak while on sightseeing flight on 3/26/72. Two died and one was seriously injured in crash. (G.P. Macha) Region 3.

Portero, killing the pilot. Site is unmarked in the Santa Ana Mountains. Other reports place this wreck south of Highway 74 on east slope above Lake Elsinore.

1953. *Grumman F9F-5 USMC* hit Galivan Peak south of Lake Matthews. Site is 100' from summit on north slope near big boulder. Pilot died in crash. Wreck is scattered and mostly removed.

Date unknown. Two *North American SNJ US Navy Reserve trainers* crashed in a rugged area of Santa Ana Canyon while on a routine training flight from NAS Los Alamitos. Both aircraft hit a cloud-obscured ridge just south of the 91 Freeway, killing all aboard the two aircraft. Wreckage is removed.

Date unknown. *Douglas AD Skyraider USMC* crashed near Sand Canyon Reservoir in the San Joaquin Hills. Wreck is unmarked and covered over.

3/24/54. *McDonnell F2H USMC* crashed in Ladd Canyon near Mustang Spring of Santa Ana Mountains. The pilot died in this bad weather-related accident. This site is unmarked and scattered.

3/10/54. *Lightplane* crashed on Pleasants Peak in the Santa Ana Mountains. No other information available. Site may be *Luscombe NC-77912* reported east of Santiago Peak

Date unknown. *Beechcraft SNB-5 USMC* crashed and burned west of Santiago Peak. The wreck itself is not marked, but a large outcropping of blue granite is painted with a yellow X.

Date unknown. *Grumman F9F USMC* crashed NE of Silverado in the Santa Ana Mountains, following pilot bailout. Wreckage is scattered and unmarked.

4/18/57. *USMC jet aircraft* crashed in mountains east of San Juan Capistrano.

1/10/58. *Douglas F3D USMC* crashed in bad weather 2.5 miles east of Highways 101 and 74. Both crewmen died in the crash, and all wreckage was removed.

1/26/58. *Douglas F3D USMC* hit the Santa Ana Mountains in bad weather fifteen miles east of El Toro, killing both crewmen.

12/14/61. *Douglas C-47 USAF* crashed in Hagador Canyon on the east slope of the Santa Ana Mountains. Three men died when their Air Force Reserve aircraft went down in bad weather. This site is marked and visible.

9/17/62. *Ercoupe N93758* crashed on Trabuco Mesa, killing both persons on board. Though unmarked, this wreck is still visible today.

1/7/63. *Grumman TBM N7833C* crash-landed while on a fire-fighting mission near Trabuco in the Santa Ana Mountain foothills. The pilot survived uninjured. The wreckage was removed.

1/31/63. *Cessna 150 N6584T* crashed at the 3,500' level of Sitton Peak in the Santa Ana Mountains. The pilot was killed in this bad weather-related accident.

5/29/63. *Lockheed T2V-1 #44149 US Navy* crashed in cloudy weather in Harding Canyon in the Santa Ana Mountains. This wreck site is unmarked and scattered. The pilot and his passenger died in the crash.

2/20/64. *Sailplane N3360E* hit near Ortega Summit at the 3,100' level, killing the pilot. Only a few parts remain at this unmarked site.

9/18/64. *Lockheed T-33 #52-9670 USAF* crashed in La Paz Canyon east of Highway 74. Wreckage is scattered and marked.

1/2/65. *Piper Cherokee N5706N* crashed in Coldwater Canyon while engaged in a Civil Air Patrol search mission. Both persons on board survived and were rescued by helicopter. Wreck is intact and probably removed.

4/11/65. *Beechcraft Baron N8522M* hit Squaw Mountain in bad weather, killing all five persons on board. Wreck is burned, but tail assembly is intact.

6/13/65. *Cessna 120 or 140* is still visible in Eagle Canyon in the Santa Ana Mountains. Wreck is unmarked in this accident which the pilot survived.

6/25/65. *Boeing C-135B USAF* enroute from El Toro Marine Corps Air Station to Hickham Air Force Base in Hawaii crashed shortly after takeoff at 1:47 am, killing all eighty-four servicemen on board. The C-135B hit a 1,350' ridge four miles NE of El Toro and exploded on impact. The tail cartwheeled over the ridge top, coming to rest on the east slope. Wreck is unmarked and 98 percent removed.

Lockheed T2V-1 #44149 US Navy

Lost on 5/29/63 killing both crewman. Photo depicts main landing gear leg and tail hook. (G.P. Macha) Region 3.

4/3/66. *Luscombe 8A N1283K* crashed in Silverado Canyon, seriously injuring both persons on board. Wreckage has been removed.

5/4/66. *Cessna 150 N8258S* crashed near town of Silverado, killing the pilot. This weather-related wreck has been removed.

7/3/66. *Temco Swift* crashed and burned south of Santiago Peak, killing both persons on board. Wreck is located in upper Holy Jim Canyon and is partly salvaged.

1/15/67. *Cessna 150 N69119* crashed in Coldwater Canyon in the Santa Ana Mountains. Both persons on board survived and this plane has been removed.

3/31/67. *Cessna 172 N7172T* crashed in bad weather at the 4,200' level of east Santiago Peak, killing two persons on board. Wreckage is marked and visible.

4/16/67. *Navion F N91734* crashed and burned at 4,500' level of Santiago Peak, killing all four men on board. This was a Civil Air Patrol search aircraft engaged in over-flying the recently discovered Cessna 172 that crashed on 3/31/67. *Wreckage* located on east slope of Santa Ana Mountains just NW of the C-172.

4/16/67. *Bell UH-1E USMC* crashed on the SW slope of Santiago Peak at 4,500' level while attempting to reach the downed Navion on the east slope. Four US Marines were killed in this weather-related accident. Wreck has been removed.

7/7/67. *Taylorcraft BC-1265 N29751* crashed in a canyon SW of Corona. The pilot escaped with minor injuries and wreck has been removed.

7/28/68. *Sikorsky UH-34D USMC* crashed and burned in Black Star Canyon of the Santa Ana Mountains, killing two and seriously injuring one crewman. Few parts remain at this site today.

1/13/69. *McDonnell Douglas RF-4B USMC* hit Sitton Peak in the Santa Ana Mountains, killing one crewman and seriously injuring another. This wreck is unmarked and scattered. Weather was a factor in this crash.

2/11/69. *Lockheed SP-2E #131487 of the US Navy Reserve* crashed while doing touch and goes at USMC Air Station, El Toro. Heavy clouds obscured

Lockheed T2V-1 #44149

Control surface from Lockheed T2V-1. (G.P. Macha) Region 3.

the Santa Ana Mountains at the time of the accident. All seven crewmen were killed on impact at the 2,800' level of Santiago Canyon. Most of this wreck has been removed, but large amounts of unmarked debris remain.

6/23/69. *Cessna 182 N6259A* crashed in cloudy weather south of Signal Peak in San Joaquin Hills. All four persons were killed. This wreck was not located until 6/28/69, even though it was only 2.5 miles from Pacific Coast Highway.

8/16/69. *Cessna 150 N8319C* crashed in the Santa Ana Mountains SW of Corona, killing both men on board. Wreck has been removed.

3/2/71. *Cessna 185* crashed in bad weather SW of Corona in foothills, killing two men. Wreck has been removed.

8/5/71. *Cessna 150 N6036D* hit a ridge south of Sitton Peak. Wreckage is red/white and visible.

2/12/72. *Sailplane* hit Elsinore Peak in clear air turbulence, killing the pilot. Wreck is removed.

3/26/72. *Cessna 172 N2619L* crashed one mile west of Santiago Peak, killing two and seriously injuring one in another pilot error-related accident. Wreckage has been removed.

9/10/73. *Cessna 172* crashed in Santiago Canyon near town of Silverado, killing both persons on board. Wreck has been removed.

11/22/74. *Beechcraft 18* crashed at night in poor weather, killing all three men on board. A few parts remain of this burned wreck above Weir Canyon in the Santa Ana Mountains.

12/27/74. A *Lightplane* crashed twelve miles south of Lake Elsinore. Both persons on board survived with serious injuries.

2/18/75. *Sikorsky CH-53 USMC* collided with another helicopter and crashed in Modjeska Canyon in the Santa Ana Mountains, killing all four crewmen. Wreck is removed.

9/26/75. A *Convair C-131 US Navy* crashed eight miles SE of El Toro Marine Air Station following a control malfunction. Four men died and two survived this accident in low rolling hills. All wreckage was removed.

11/16/75. A *Cessna 172* crashed in hills near Laguna Niguel in cloudy weather. All four persons on board survived with minor injuries.

5/9/76. *Cessna 172 N35325* crashed in Fremont Canyon in the Santa Ana Mountains in cloudy weather. All three persons on board survived. Wreck has been removed.

5/29/76. *Cessna 172 N12227.* One man died in lightplane crash in Hagador Canyon in the Santa Ana Mountains. Weather was a factor in this accident.

10/9/76. *Aero Commander N1450J* crashed in Holy Jim Canyon near Santiago Peak, killing the only person on board. Weather was a factor in this accident.

7/13/77. *Cessna 150* crashed near town of Silverado, killing both men on board. Status of this site today is unknown.

8/25/77. *Bell UH-1 USMC* crashed and burned in Trabuco Canyon, seriously injuring all six men on board.

Date unknown. *Piper PA-24 Commanche N6295T* lies wrecked in the Santa Margarita Mountains SE of San Clemente.

8/31/77. *Lightplane* crashed and burned in the mountains SW of Corona, killing all four on board. Weather was a factor in this accident.

3/3/78. *Bell UH-1N USMC* hit trees while on rescue mission in Trabuco Canyon. One man was seriously injured and four men escaped with minor injuries. Wreck is removed.

4/15/78. *Piper Aztec N5641Y* piloted by Frank Tallman of aviation stunt and movie fame crashed at the 3,500' level of Santiago Peak in Holy Jim Canyon. Tallman was killed in this late-night, weather-related accident. Wreckage removed from site by helicopter. Tallman had logged more than 21,000 flight hours at the time of his death.

3/30/81. *Cessna 172 N738WD* crashed in hills SW of Temecula. Wreck is reported removed.

1/13/84. *Cessna 182 N9456H* crashed at night in Gypsum Canyon, one mile south of the 91 Freeway. All three persons on board were killed. Wreckage is scattered and some parts are visible.

4/9/84. *Piper Tomahawk N2314P* upside down on Three Sisters Mountain in canyon south of Woodcrest.

3/6/86. *Robinson R-2* made a crash landing near summit of Santiago Peak. Both occupants survived with minor injuries. Wreck has been removed.

3/15/86 *McDonnell Douglas OA-4M USMC* landed intact in Sheep Hills, following successful crew ejection after an inflight malfunction. Wreck is removed.

11/14/86. *Bell Textron AH-1T USMC* crashed in bad weather near San Juan Hot Springs in the Santa Ana Mountains. Both crewmen were killed on impact.

2/12/87. *Boeing Vertol CH-46E USMC* crashed at 2,300' level of the Santa Ana Mountains in bad weather. All three crewmen were killed. Only a few parts remain visible at the site which is located near Trabuco Canyon.

8/14/88. *Bell Textron UH-1H of the US Army Reserve* crashed in rugged Bell Canyon, injuring two crewmen. The aircraft was destroyed by fire following the forced landing during a night training mission.

Luscombe 8A N1283K crashed in Silverado Canyon of the Santa Ana Mountains on 4/3/66 seriously injuring both persons on board. (NTSB) Region 3.

11/9/88. *Piper Cherokee* crashed in the Santa Ana Mountains three miles east of Irvine Lake. One person was killed and two were seriously injured. Wreckage has been removed.

2/19/89. *Cessna 402 N69383* on a flight from Las Vegas to John Wayne Airport crashed at 2,100' level of Hagador Canyon in the Santa Ana Mountains. All ten persons on board were killed. Scattered parts remain at site. Stratus clouds obscured the mountains at time of crash.

2/23/90. *Cessna 152 N677558* crashed in cloudy weather east of Santiago Peak in Mayhew Canyon within several hundred yards of a Cessna 172 that crashed on 5/31/67. Both persons survived in the Cessna 152 with minor injuries. Wreck is visible. Wings are sheared off fuselage.

Date unknown. *Cessna 310* reported wrecked in Santa Ana Mountains west of Lake Elsinore. No other data available.

9/19/95. *Bell 206* hit ridge one mile SE of Irvine Lake at 1,200 level in cloudy weather. Pilot died in crash and wreck was removed.

Lockheed SP-2E #131487 USN Reserve crashed in the Santa Ana Mountains on 2/11/69 killing all seven men on board. (G.P. Macha) Region 3.

Region 4

Region 4 includes the San Jacinto Mountains and Badlands district which is bounded on the north by Interstate 10, with State Highway 111 providing the eastern boundary. The southern and western limits of this region are bordered by State Highway 79 and Interstate 215. The highest point in this region is 10,786' Mt.San Jacinto. About forty crash sites are located within this region of both timber forests and rugged chaparral.

3/30/29. *Fokker Tri-motor of New Standard Airlines* crashed in bad weather near Beaumont. Four persons were killed in this accident. Some small parts remain at the site, which is located in the Badlands.

12/18/40. *Boeing Y1B-17 #36-157 USAAC* crashed near Marion Mountain Camp killing all six crewmen. Weather was a factor in this accident. Small parts still litter the forest floor only 200 yards above the Marion Mountain Trail.

(For further details on 12/18/40 crash please see inset MAP next page)

10/23/42. *Douglas DC-3 American Airlines NC-16017* crashed following a mid-air collision in Chino Canyon near Palm Springs. Many unmarked parts litter the crash site to this day. The *USAAC Bomber* involved in this accident landed safely.

9/24/43. *Ryan PT-22 USAAF #41-5748* crashed, killing the student pilot in mountains SE of Hemet. This wreck remained undisturbed until 1975 when an aircraft parts restorer removed most of the wreckage from the Rouse Hill site

Date unknown. A *Consolidated B-24 USAAF* hit Mt.Russell in cloudy weather while operating from March Army Air Field. The wreckage is 98 percent removed.

Date unknown. *Vultee BT-13 USAAF* crashed near Tahquitz Peak in the San Jacinto Mountains. This site is unmarked and burned.

Date unknown. *Vultee BT-13 USAAF* crashed SW of Palm Springs near Tahquitz Peak. Status of site is unknown.

12/18/40. *Boeing Y1B-17 #36-157 USAAC* crash site in the San Jacinto Mountains north of Idyllwild. Take State Road 243 to Marion Mountain Campground. Park here and take the Marion Mountain trail east for about ten to fifteen minutes walking time. The crash site is about 200 yards above the trail in heavy woods. Scattered B-17 parts are visible 100' above the trail, while the main impact site is near large boulders. 90% of this wreck has been removed but it's still a worthwhile walk into the past. Please refrain from taking anything from this rare old Flying Fortress. The time to visit this site is from May through October.

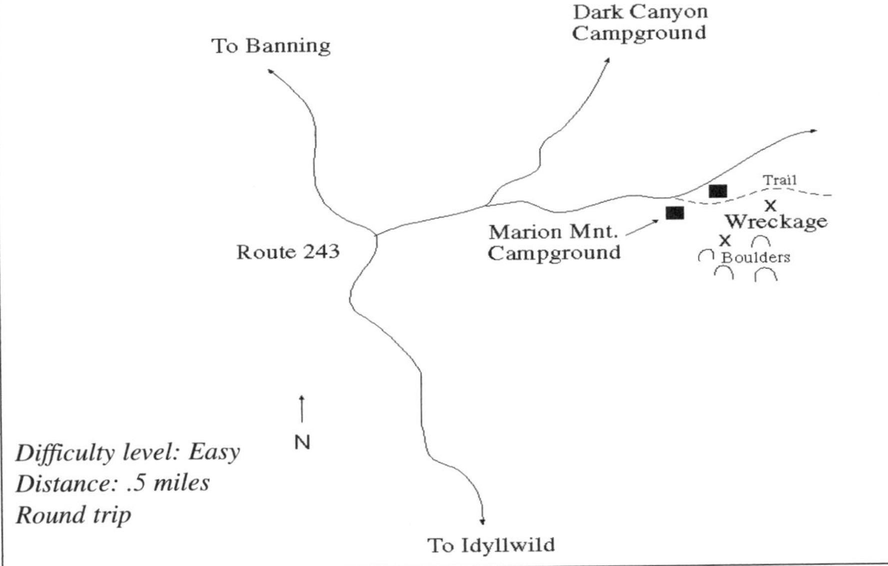

Difficulty level: Easy
Distance: .5 miles
Round trip

Date unknown. *Fairchild PT-26 NC-60506* crashed on the north slope of Palm View Peak. Wreckage is unmarked and is also reported south of Bonito Vista Ranch.

Date unknown. *Fairchild PT-19 N48588* in hills NE of the town of San Jacinto. Wreck is unmarked. Both persons survived this accident and the aircraft remained intact and undisturbed until the early 1980s. Today only a few small parts remain.

Date unknown. *Vultee BT-13 NC62556* crashed on the east slope of the San Jacinto Mountains just below the ridge line near Palm View Peak. This wreck is marked and hard to see from the air.

Date unknown. *Aeronca NC-83776* is on Pyramid Peak. This wreck was unmarked and undisturbed for several years until it was discovered by deer hunters in the mid 1950s. One man died in this accident.

4/7/51. *Bellanca NC-73349* crashed in bad weather, killing all three persons on board. This wreck is located in the Badlands and is marked.

Date unknown. *Douglas AD-4N US Navy of Squadron VR-35* is in steep canyon SE of Idyllwild. Only tail assembly and small parts remain at site today and this is visible from "white post curve" on Highway 74.

8/13/54. *North American F-51D California Air National Guard* crashed on Double Butte west of town of Hemet, killing the pilot. Aircraft was observed to have broken up while engaged in aerobatics. Wreckage was consumed by fire, leaving only a few scattered parts on the NW slope of Double Butte.

Date unknown. *Douglas C-47 USAF* hit the Box Springs Mountains at the 2,300' level, killing all on board. Only a few scattered parts remain at site.

Date unknown. *Boeing C-97 USAF.* crashed in Box Springs Mountains while operating from March AFB All perished in this weather-related crash.

The author and Dan Hammer with wreck of Vultee BT-13 NC62556 near Palm View Peak. (P.J. Macha) Region 4.

Wreck is mostly removed, but propeller blades and small parts remain.

5/12/59. *Light plane* crashed on Pinion Flats near Asbestos Peak in bad weather. Both persons on board survived with only minor injuries.

6/22/61. *Grumman TBM* crashed while on a fire-fighting mission at the 3,000' level of Billy Goat Mountain south of Hemet. The pilot was killed and the aircraft wreckage is scattered and burned.

2/28/62. *Cessna 175 N6522E* hit One Horse Ridge north of Mt. San Jacinto in bad weather, killing all three people on board. Wreckage visible and not marked.

5/4/62. *Cessna 195 N3065B* crashed in cloudy weather on Fuller Ridge of Mt. San Jacinto, killing three persons on board. This wreck is scattered and unmarked.

7/23/62. *Grumman TBM N5170V* crashed while on a fire-fighting mission in the Badlands SW of Beaumont, killing the pilot. Scattered parts remain at site.

Date unknown. *Military helicopter* crashed on Black Mountain north of Idyllwild. Status unknown.

Date unknown. *Lightplane* wreckage is reported north of Idyllwild near Marion Mountain Camp. No other data available.

2/16/65. *Douglas A-4E USMC* crashed and burned near Lake Hemet. The pilot died in crash. Wreckage is unmarked and scattered.

3/19/66. *Stearman PT-17 N59792* hit Mt. Russell in cloudy weather, killing the pilot. Crash site is near Sunnymead at 1,950' level and wreckage has been removed.

7/20/68. *Grumman TBM-3 N9679C* exploded on impact while on a fire-fighting mission four miles SW of Idyllwild next to Highway 74. The pilot was killed and many unmarked parts remain at site above the road, a few miles east of Cranston Forest service station.

1/21/69. *Cessna 337 N2512S* hit Mt. San Jacinto's east slope at 3,700' level. All three persons on board perished in this winter storm crash. Wreckage is scattered and marked near Mt. Edna.

11/2/69. *Cessna 150 N4783X* hit Cahuilla Mountain SE of Hemet, killing both persons on board. Weather was a factor in this accident.

4/22/71. *Cessna 172* crashed 5.5 miles south of Banning at 4,000' level. Accident occurred in bad weather, killing both persons in the plane. This wreck is visible and marked.

6/9/71. *Ryan Navion* crashed in bad weather ten miles west of Banning in Badlands, killing both persons on board.

10/8/72. *Beechcraft Bonanza* crashed in San Timateo Canyon west of Banning, killing all four on board.

3/31/74. *Cessna 150 N16028* hit Palm View Peak in clear air turbulence.

Grumman TBM-3 N9679C

An aviation archaeologist in his own right, Romano Urbat pauses beside the Wright R-2600 engine belonging to Grumman TBM-3. (R. Urbat) Region 4.

Tail assembly and borate tank of Grumman TBM-3 N9679C that crashed on 7/20/68. (P. J. Macha) Region 4.

The pilot escaped with minor injuries. No other data available.

9/9/74. *Pitts Special* crashed in the Box Springs Mountains, killing the pilot. Wreckage is removed.

8/15/75. *Police helicopter* crashed on Tahquitz Peak, killing one man and seriously injuring another.

4/15/76. *Beechcraft 99* hit Black Hill at 3,869' level in cloudy weather, killing all six persons on board. Wreckage removed from site south of Hemet.

Date unknown. *Cessna 172* is unmarked in heavy chaparral east of Angelus Hill Road in the bottom of draw. Wreckage is red and white and very hard to see. 33° 48'N 116° 52'W.

3/22/78. *Cessna 207* crashed in Box Springs Mountains, killing six people on board. Weather was a factor in this accident.

12/5/82. *Cessna 172 N737LA* listed unmarked east of Tahquitz Peak.

6/12/88. *Luscombe Sedan* crashed at 5,000' level of Mt. San Jacinto. None of the four persons on board was seriously injured. Wreckage is located near the Palm Springs Aerial Tram.

Date unknown. *Cessna 150 N3357E* is listed wrecked in San Jacinto Mountains SW of Palm Springs. No other data available.

11/90. *Piper Lance N711PE* hit granite wall 500 yards NW of Palm Springs and exploded, killing the pilot. Wreck is unmarked and scattered.

12/7/91. *Home built aircraft* crashed and burned, killing the pilot in the Badlands west of Beaumont.

1/8/93. *Cessna 172 N20513* crashed south of Mt. San Jacinto summit. The pilot survived and was rescued by helicopter. Wreck is unmarked.

2/24/94. *Cessna 150* crashed at the 2,500' level of a mountain two miles north of the Soboda Indian Reservation. Both pilot and passenger died in this weather-related accident. Wreck is unmarked.

3/22/96. *Piper Cherokee* crashed, killing both occupants in the Box Springs Mountains at the 2,000' level. Wreck is mostly removed.

Tail of Mooney Mk 21 N3624H that vanished 8/5/83 and was not found until 11/21/91. (J. Zimmerman) Region 5.

Tony Moore (left) and Peter Merlin of the Archeology Field Research Team, better known as "The X-Hunters" at the crash site of the X-15 56-6672 lost on 11/15/67. (Peter Merlin) Region 5.

Region 5

Region 5 is characterized as a classic example of basin and range topography. This area includes the Mojave Desert and a dozen minor mountain ranges, including the Little San Bernardino, Providence, Bullion, Bristol, Ord, Avawatz, and Old Woman Mountains. The highest peak in this region is 7,929' Clark Mountain, located north of Interstate 15 near the Nevada Border. In this vast and often forbidding expanse lie the remains of more than 130 aircraft.

This book lists only a few of the dozens of aircraft that crashed in and around Edwards Air Force Base. Peter Merlin and Tony Moore, the "X-Hunters," who search for the remains of experimental aircraft in this region, will soon publish a comprehensive, detailed book that will address the mishaps and losses at this historic base. In the meantime those who explore the challenging topography of the Great Mojave Desert will continue to discover its secrets.

Date unknown. *Curtiss P-40N USAAF* crashed on training flight near highway 395 north of Victorville. Pilot was from Chinese Air Force and he died in crash.

8/24/29. *Lockheed Vega R393H* crashed in bad weather near Randsburg, killing the pilot. Wreckage burned.

9/2/29. *Lockheed Vega C859E* went down in a violent thunderstorm north of Needles, killing the pilot and injuring a passenger. Status of wreck unknown.

1940-41. *North American O-47 USAAC* unmarked parts and Wright R-1820-49 engine are visible near the town of Rice south of Highway 62.

12/19/40. *North American Harvard I* disappeared on a delivery flight to Royal Canadian Air Force. Wreck was not located until 1/17/42 in Ivanpah Mountains with the pilot's remains still on board. Site is north of Cima, east of Kessler Springs in Box Canyon.

12/12/41. *Douglas DC-3 (?)* There have been many inquiries regarding the so called "Diamond DC-3" as described in *Treasure Magazine* and other publications. The story in brief states that a wealthy Los Angeles businessman, fearing a Japanese attack on the West Coast, chartered a DC-3 at Mines Field to carry himself and some $250 thousand in diamonds to safety in Utah. The last alleged radio contact was near Barstow, California. The plane disappeared without a trace, and to this day has not been found. No record of this event has been discovered. The DC-3 registry information reveals no data whatsoever to support this story. Still "the legend" spreads among desert aficionados and for some of these folks, the search goes on in spite of the apparent facts.

3/13/42. *Curtiss AT-9 USAAF* crashed in desert near Dobe Corners south of Victorville. One bailed out and one died in the crash. Wreck is mostly removed.

3/17/43. *Boeing B-17E USAAF* crashed and burned west of Blythe, killing all on board.

5/28/43. Two *US Army planes* collided near Silver Lake 90 miles NE of Victorville. One aircraft crashed and burned, killing all four men on board. Some unmarked debris is reported at site today.

Vultee BT-15 #42-1833 USAAF

Located in Pinto Mtns. south of Twenty-Nine Palms. Pilot died on training mission during WW ll. (P. J. Macha) Region 5.

6/2/43. A *Consolidated B-24* crashed ten miles east of Inyokern following successful crew bailout.

1943-44. *Vultee BT-15 #42-1833 USAAC* wreck is located in the Pinto Mountains south of Twentynine Palms. This site is burned and marked with yellow X's.

3/29/45. *Consolidated B-24 USAAF* reported five miles south of Kramer Junction east of Highway 395.

1940s. *North American T-6* wreckage is located in the eastern part of Joshua Tree National Monument. Site is unmarked and burned.

Date unknown. *North American A-36A USAAF* lies scattered in the Fenner Hills. Wreck was not located until late 1950s. Site is unmarked.

1940s. *Consolidated PBY US Navy* crashed in the Cady Mountains NE of Barstow. This site is marked and highly visible.

Date unknown. *Bell P-39 USAAF* crashed at SW edge of Amboy Crater in lava and is unmarked.

1940s. *North American P-51D #44-73698 USAAF* is located in Providence Mountains. Site is unmarked.

Date unknown. *Bell P-39 USAAF*. crashed in desert 15 miles south of Rice AAB following mid-air collision.

1944. *Lockheed P-38L #44-24790 USAAF* is burned and unmarked in the Soda Mountains.

2/17/44. *Vought F4U-1A USMC* crashed in SE end of the Slate Range, killing the pilot. Wreck is marked.

3/30/44. (2) *Vought F4U-1A USMC* aircraft based at USMCAS Mojave collided while engaged in aerial target practice at 18,000'. One *F4U-1A* ran into not only the tow target, but the tow plane as well, resulting in a fatal flat spin for #17562. The pilot of the tow *F4U-1A* parachuted to safety moments before his plane hit the Slate Mountains and exploded. Extensive salvage work was done on the tow plane, possibly for metal value, only in the 1950s. *F4U-1A #17562* is virtually intact and untouched in a small wash about one mile from the "high site." The engine of #17562 lies by itself midway between the wrecks, having been wrenched off the fuselage by the force of the collision and subsequent entanglement with the tow banner and cable. These sites are unmarked SW of Trona and may be on the border or just within the property of China Lake Naval Test Center.

6/1/44. *Lockheed P-38 USAAF* crashed in Wingate Pass near Owl Dry Lake. Status of wreck is unknown.

Date unknown. *Lockheed P-38 USAAF* N.E. of Black Butte east of Palmdale.

1943-44. *North American B-25C USAAF* lies burned and scattered east of Grey Butte Airfield, west of Highway 395.

7/14/44. *Bell P-63A #42-69034* crashed fifteen miles SW of Muroc, killing the pilot. Wreck is removed.

1940s. *North American AT-6 (AT-16) #42-913* is burned and unmarked north of Interstate 15 near the Nevada border.

Date unknown. *Old aircraft wreckage* is reported on the west face of Cedar Canyon north of Kelso in the Mid Hills.

10/12/47. *Stinson NC-591000* is located near Interstate 15 in Ivanpah Mountains. Site is unmarked.

10/21/47. *Northrop P-61C #42-8322 USAF* on loan to Northrop Aircraft for use as a photo plane in YB-49 test program crashed following in-flight fire that forced the three man crew to bailout at 12,000'. P-61C spun in and burned twenty-five miles east of Palmdale and several miles south of Black Butte. Wreck is mostly removed.

12/3/48. *Douglas C-47 USAF* crashed, killing four men, 25 miles east of Edwards AFB.

4/4/51. *North American F-51D #356 of the California Air National Guard* lies wrecked NW of Barstow.

Date unknown. *Culver PQ-14 #442259 USAF* intact at 35° 44'N 116° 44'W. Reported burned in the 1960s.

Date Unknown. Two *Douglas B-26 USAF* collided and crashed west of Adelanto in Victor Valley. Wreckage is mostly removed.

1950s. *North American F-86 USAF* crashed in Little San Bernardino Mountains. Site is scattered and unmarked 116° 11 1/2'W 33° 55'N.

1950s. *Aeronca Sedan* wreck is located near Mountain Pass just west of Nevada border. Pilot died trying to walk out to highway. Site is unmarked.

1950s. *Cessna 195* wreck is located NE of Barstow in mountains. Site is unmarked.

Date unknown. A *Douglas AD-1* lies wrecked in the Hidalgo Mountains within USMC Training Center, Twentynine Palms. Wreck is marked.

1950s. *North American Navion NC-4345* lies marked in Shadow Mountains north of Interstate 15.

1950s. *Luscombe 8* is burned and unmarked north of Interstate 15 near Baker.

1950s. *Military jet fighter* is scattered and unmarked north of Barstow on US Navy test range.

12/16/61 Lockheed 12 N16020 crashed at 1,300' level of the Tiefort Mtn. killing both men on board. Site is near Bicycle Lake on Fort Irwin. (Bob Buhrle) Region 5.

1950s. *Sikorsky HRS-2 US Navy* lies wrecked and marked in Shadow Mountains.

12/12/57. *Lockheed T-33 USAF* scattered near Rosamond Dry Lake. Pilot killed following mid-air collision.

12/28/57. *Lockheed T-33A USAF* crashed near 4,131' peak in Whipple Mountains following pilot ejection. Wreck is scattered and marked on NW face.

2/12/58. *Lockheed T-33A USAF* crashed eight miles north of Lucerne Valley in the Granite Mountains. Pilot died in crash. Small unmarked parts reported at site today.

2/28/58. *Lockheed T-33A USAF* crashed four miles south of Atolia, killing both crewmen. Status of wreck is unknown.

1/31/59. *Douglas B-26 USAF* is visible in Old Dad Mountains. Tail is intact and unmarked in wash three miles north of Interstate 40. Mid-air collision was cause of crash. Site of main impact is unknown.

11/2/59. *Cessna 182 N2578G* colored yellow and black is located north of Interstate 15 near Nevada border. This aircraft was missing for seventy-five days and was discovered as search planes were looking for another missing plane. Wreck is unmarked in Yucca trees and rocks in the Clark Mountains.

11/29/59. *Beechcraft Bonanza N3989N* is unmarked and burned just off the Kelbaker Road at 3,400' level in Granite Mountains.

12/10/59. *Douglas A-4B #142845 US Navy* is burned and unmarked in Joshua Tree National Monument. Pilot died in crash.

9/8/60. *Luscombe 8E* hit peak north of Apple Valley, killing both persons on board. Status of wreck is not known.

6/23/61. *Grumman TF-9J #147380 US Navy* disappeared with two men on board. Wreckage was not located until 12/19/61 in Indio Canyon in the Joshua Tree National Monument. This wreck is scattered and unmarked.

Date unknown. *Douglas A-4 US Navy* crashed in the Cady Mountains north of Highway 40. Wreck is scattered.

11/18/61. *Howard DGA N144* lies in flat brushy area south of Interstate 40, at 34° 51'N 115° 01'W. Unmarked fuselage frame remains at crash site.

12/4/61. *Cessna 180 N2089G* is scattered and unmarked in McCoy Mountains north of Interstate 10. Wreckage not located until 2/25/63.

12/16/61. *Lockheed 12 N16020* hit the 1,300' level of Tiefort Mountain near Bicycle Lake on Fort Irwin. Two men died in this accident. Wreck is burned but tail is intact.

11/10/62. *Cessna 182 N6389A* is scattered in Alvord Mountains north of Interstate 15.

1963. *Military airplane* south of Interstate 40 in Marble Mountains. Wreckage is scattered.

2/18/63. *Piper PA-28 N2147P* is located in desert west of Barstow, and may be removed.

4/12/63. *Lockheed F-104 #86896 USAF* lies scattered in Soda Mountains north of Interstate 15.

4/12/63. *Bell OH-13G* is located in Soda Mountains north of Interstate 15. Wreckage visible and unmarked.

1/1/64. *Douglas A-4 US Navy* is visible and marked north of Interstate 40 near the Cady Mountains.

2/11/64. *North American F-100 USAF* is scattered in Alvord Mountains north of Interstate 15.

6/8/64. *Beechcraft Bonanza N3730N* crashed and burned in bad weather near Ludlow, killing all three persons on board. Wreck is burned and unmarked.

7/8/64. *Republic F-105 and Boeing KC-135, USAF* aircraft, collided while engaged in in-flight re-fueling. One man aboard the F-105 was killed, and four men aboard the KC-135 died. F-105 wreckage is at north end of Owl Dry Lake near Fort Irwin. KC-135 wreckage is scattered at the southern end of Death Valley National Monument.

1964. *Douglas A-4 Navy/Marine Reserve* crashed in Bristol Mountains north of Interstate 40. This site is marked and visible.

Date unknown. *Grumman F6F-5K USN* drone lies scattered and unmarked in the Argus Mountains west of Trona.

Date unknown. *Grumman-F6F-5K USN* drone crashed in the Spangler Hills south of Ridgecrest. Small unmarked parts remain at the site.

Date unknown. *Sikorsky H-34* lies wrecked and unmarked north of Interstate 40 west of the community of Mountain Pass.

1/9/65. *Piper Apache N3251P* crashed landed in Lucerne Valley. Both persons on board escaped with minor injuries. This wreck has been removed.

5/22/65. *Cessna 172 N3825* crashed at the 4,000' level in the Old Woman Mountains fifty-five miles west of Needles. Two people died in the accident and the wreck was not found until 3/20/66.

11/16/65. *Lear Jet N243F* hit the Little San Bernardino Mountains, killing all eight persons on board. This wreck is burned and scattered, but not marked.

12/17/65. *Lockheed T-33A USAF* crashed in the Clipper Mountains following

The author and tail section of a F4U-1A #17562 which crashed S.E. of Trona. (P. J. Macha) Region 5.

the pilot's ejection in a heavy snowstorm. The pilot walked to Interstate 40 for help. The wreck is still highly visible and marked at 34° 45'N 115° 23' W. Site is 4,000' M.S.L.

6/8/66. *Lockheed F-104 NASA* mid-air collision with *North American Rockwell XB-70 #62-0000 USAF*, in which two men died and one survived, rained wreckage on the Mojave Desert. Parts of these aircraft can still be seen over a wide area twelve miles north of Barstow and one mile NW of FAA radar site on Velvet Mountain.

8/18/66. *Douglas A-4C US Navy* lies scattered fifteen miles NW of town of Ludlow, off Interstate 40. 34° 46'N 116° 19'W.

2/20/67. *McDonnell F-4C #65-0656 USAF* crashed in the Shadow Mountains. This site is burned and marked.

Date unknown. *Piper PA-28* is reported unmarked on Iron Mountain west of Barstow.

5/18/67. *McDonnell F-4D #65-668 USAF* lies in the Devil's Playground. Wreckage is burned and marked.

Date unknown. *North American F-100 USAF* is visible and marked at 35° 42'N 116° 57'W.

5/18/67. *McDonnell F-4 USAF* crashed and burned north of Edwards AFB. This site is marked.

Date unknown. *Ryan Firebee #KD-4591 USN* lies wrecked in the Argus Range west of Trona. Drone color is grey and unmarked.

7/10/67. *McDonnell F-4* is burned and marked west of Barstow on Iron Mountain.

Date unknown. *Ryan Firebee USN* drone is unmarked in lower Slate Range. Aircraft color is faded orange and white.

11/2/67. *Temco Swift N231C* is wrecked south of Afton in Cady Mountains near Interstate 15. Status of site today is unknown.

Date unknown. *North American QF-86F* target drone crashed on Searles Dry Lake east of Trona. Wreck is mostly removed but some unmarked parts remain of this Japanese built F-86F.

11/15/67. *North American X-15 #56-6672 USAF* crashed after hypersonic spin a few miles north of Johannesburg. Small unmarked parts remain.

Date unknown. *Sailplane* wreckage reported in Indio Hills NW of Indio.

12/8/67. *Lockheed F-104D USAF* crashed twenty-eight miles NE of Edwards AFB, killing the pilot.

Date unknown. *Cessna 172 N12563* wrecked east of Cima in Mid Hills.

1/19/69. *Cessna 172 N79103* crashed, killing the pilot, twenty-eight miles west of Needles. N79103 went down in bad weather while on delivery flight from Kansas to California. Wreck is burned and unmarked in the Piute Mountains.

5/18/69. *Cessna 170 N3281A* crashed in sand dunes north of Highway 40.

9/28/69. *Cessna 170B N2583D* crashed sixteen miles NW of Needles near Homer Mountain. All four persons on board survived and were rescued.

10/23/69. *Douglas TA-4F #153666 US Navy* crashed in mountains south of Yucca Valley. No other information available.

11/9/69. *Cessna 205 N81942* hit a mountain eight miles SW of Twentynine Palms. One person died in this weather-related crash. Wreck is burned and unmarked.

Date unknown. *Grumman F9F-5KD US Navy* colored orange scattered and unmarked on unnamed peak in southern end of Slate Range. Aircraft was a target drone flown from NWC China Lake.

2/10/70. *McDonnell Douglas F-4E #68-0356* crashed in Providence Mountains at 4,000' level. Both USAF officers were killed in crash.

Date unknown. *General Dynamics F-106A USAF* hit Pilot Knob east of Johannesburg on NWC China Lake. Wreck is unmarked and scattered.

6/22/70. *McDonnell Douglas F-4E #66285 USAF* is scattered and unmarked ten miles north of Edwards AFB.

Date unknown. *Cessna wreckage* reported SE of Ivanpah at north end of Lanfair Valley.

3/18/71. *US Navy jet trainer* crashed nineteen miles NW of Blythe, killing the only crewman on board.

Date unknown. *Beechcraft 35 N6641S* wrecked on Fry Mountain NE Lucerne Valley.

4/24/71. *General Dynamics F-111E #66-117 USAF* crashed south of Death Valley near Owl Dry Lake. Both USAF officers perished when their escape system failed.

6/71. *Martin B-57B USAF* crashed fifteen miles north of Edwards AFB. Both crewmen were killed.

1/16/73. *Lightplane* crashed in Joshua Tree National Monument, killing all three people on board.

3/6/73. *McDonnell F-101B #58-0278 USAF* crashed ten miles SW of Barstow in rugged terrain. This site is visible and marked.

6/14/73. *Piper PA-28 N4806L* crashed in mountains south of Twentynine Palms. Red and white wreckage is visible.

6/25/74. *Northrop F-5E #72-01397 USAF*. crashed fifteen miles north of Boron.

4/16/75. *McDonnell Douglas RF-4C #64-1025 USAF* crashed near Haystack Butte on Edwards AFB.

Date unknown. *Northrop QT-38A USN* lies scattered and unmarked in mountains west of Trona in the Argus Range.

3/8/75. *Rockwell International Shrike Commander N711lZ* crashed at 5,000' level of Providence Mountains on Fountain Peak. Both persons on board were killed.

6/22/75. *Stinson* crashed and burned SE of Twentynine Palms near Dog Wash.

3/1/76. *Cessna 401 N42J* crashed and killed all four on board ten miles NE of Desert Hot Springs. Site is located in Joshua Tree National Monument.

3/11/76. *McDonnell Douglas RF-4C #64-1002* crashed in desert near Edwards Air Force Base.

8/3/76. *McDonnell Douglas A-4F USN* crashed twenty miles SW of Needles following pilot ejection. Parts remain at 34° 35'N 114° 44'W at 1,500' level on flat desert.

12/31/76. *Beechcraft Baron N4635S* crashed thirty miles SE of Barstow, killing all four on board. Wreckage is unmarked and demolished in the Fry Mountains.

5/30/77. *Piper Cherokee* hit 5,500' mountain south of Yucca Valley, killing both persons on board. Weather was a factor in this accident.

12/25/77. *Grumman American Tiger N74787* hit hills three miles north of Desert Hot Springs in the Little San Bernardino Mountains.

9/11/78. *Boeing Vertol CH-46E USMC* crashed in the Pinto Basin of Joshua Tree National Monument. All five servicemen aboard perished.

4/26/80. *Cessna 172* crashed at 5,600' level of Piute Mountains NW of Needles. One person survived and one died in this accident.

4/15/81. *McDonnell Douglas F-4N USMC* crashed on Naval Weapons Center Mojave Range B. Wreck may be removed. No other data available.

4/18/81. *Cessna 172* near Pinto Mountain SE Twentynine Palms.

Date unknown. *Bellanca Viking* reported visible south of Vidal near Riverside Mountains.

6/1/81. *McDonnell Douglas F-4 USAF* in sand dunes SW of Kelso. Status unknown.

Date unknown. *McDonnell Douglas TA-4J USN* at east end of Rogers Dry Lake scattered and unmarked. Wing clearly visible in 1992 report.

2/11/82. *Beechcraft BE-55 N200WJ* south of Highway 62 thirty miles east of Twentynine Palms and SE of Clarks Pass.

Date unknown. *Cessna 206* lies wrecked and scattered on desert NE of Clark Pass east of Sheephole Mountains.

2/25/82. *Hughes 500 California Highway Patrol helicopter* crashed in mountains thirty-five miles NW of Barstow, killing both crewmen. Parts still visible at site.

Date unknown. *Sikorsky CH-53A USMC* is visible on flat desert west of Hidalgo Mountains. Site is on USMCTC Twentynine Palms.

3/13/82. *Cessna 182 N21409* wrecked on McCoy Mountain NW of Blythe.

11/15/82. *Grumman OV-1D US Army* crashed ten miles NW of Boron, killing both crewmen.

2/5/83. *Beechcraft Baron N1586W* hit mountains in Joshua Tree National Monument, killing two persons. Site is near Keys View.

8/5/83. *Mooney Mk. 21 N3624H* crashed three miles north of Interstate 40 near town of Fenner when pilot attempted emergency landing in bad weather at night. The aircraft disintegrated after hitting a small gully with landing gear extended, killing all three persons on board. Wreck was not located until 1/21/91 when Civil Air Patrol search planes were looking for missing Cessna 336. Entire site was cleaned up in Fall of 1993.

10/2/83. *Grumman A-6E USMC* crashed in mountains south of Twentynine Palms, killing both crewmen. Wreck is scattered, mostly removed.

Non-fatal crash on Red Mountain east of Hwy. 395. Plane is a Piper Commanche. (T. Gossett) Region 5.

6/3/84. *Piper PA-31 N6GW* crashed and burned in Kelso Mountains.

7/12/84. *Cessna* wrecked on west El Paso Peak in El Paso Mountains.

8/23/84. *Aero Commander* crashed in Calumet Mountains NE of Twentynine Palms.

8/29/84. *Rockwell International B-1A #74-0159 USAF* crashed nine miles NE of Kramer Junction following stall during low-speed/low-altitude test. The escape capsule functioned properly, but sadly one of the three-man crew was killed. Much unmarked material still litters this accident site.

9/23/84. *Piper PA-28 N8139D* in Bristol Mountains north of Interstate 40.

3/19/85. *Cessna 210 N7748K* on Clark Mountain north of Interstate 15. Wreck is unmarked.

3/28/85. A *Cessna O-2A #68-107 USAF* crashed while on routine training mission over Fort Irwin in the Avawatz Mountains. Wreckage is scattered and visible. No other data available.

12/4/87. *Beechcraft Bonanza N25MR* crashed north of Desert Center near Pinto Wells in Eagle Mountains.

4/17/88. *Piper Cherokee 140* is wrecked and marked in the Providence Mountains at the 6,800 level of Fountain Peak. Site is marked with black X's and is on east side of the mountain. At least two persons died in this crash.

5/24/88. *Mooney Mk. 21 N57694* lies scattered in Black Hills south of Inyokern.

7/22/89. *Sikorsky UH-60 US Army* crashed on Fort Irwin in the Granite Mountains while on a night training flight. Six men died and one man was seriously injured. Wreck is burned.

11/3/89. *McDonnell Douglas A-4M USMC* crashed north of Twentynine Palms near the Bullion Mountains. Pilot ejected safely following systems malfunction. Wreck is scattered and to be removed.

2/13/90. *McDonnell Douglas AV-8B USMC* crashed on the desert north of Twentynine Palms. Pilot ejected safely. Wreck is removed.

1/14/91. *Bell Textron UH-1N #69-6635 USAF* crashed during night training over northern section of Edwards AFB. Both crewmen died in crash and wreck is mostly removed.

1/26/92. *Piper PA-28 N8432K* crashed SW of Nipton. Status of wreck is unknown.

2/22/93. *Piper Commanche* crash landed on the south slope of Red Mountain near Highway 395. Both persons aboard survived with minor injuries.

7/25/93. *Beechcraft BE-33A #N3022W* disappeared on a flight from Vernal, Utah, to Camarillo, California, with three persons on board. Wreckage was not discovered until 4/29/94, thanks to the determined efforts of California Civil Air Patrol pilot Bob Buhrle. Crash site is twelve miles NE of Baker on flat desert.

6/20/95. *Cessna 172* crashed in the Whipple Mountains eighteen miles NE of Vidal Junction. Pilot died in crash.

12/23/95. *Piper Commanche N7304P* disappeared with one man on board

Message left by family member on N3624H wreckage. (J. Zimmerman) Region 5.

while transiting the Death Valley National Monument area. Wreck was not discovered until July of 1996 when a communications worker noticed the downed plane near a microwave tower sixteen miles S.E. of Furnace Creek.

10/25/96. *Piper PA-44* bound from Kingman, Arizona, to Palm Springs, California, crashed in bad weather on the north side of Indio Hills, killing both persons on board.

Mooney MK20E hit trees on ridge east of Heart Bar State Park and plunged into the upper end of Mission Creek Canyon. Two adults and a child died in this crash of 5/7/71. (G.P. Macha) Region 6.

REGION 6

Region 6 is the San Bernardino Mountains and adjacent low hills including the Crafton Hills. Located here is the highest mountain in Southern California, 11,499' Mt. San Gorgonio. More than ninety crashes have occurred here since 1911. This region is bordered on the east by Highways 62 and 247, on the west by Interstate 15E and 15, on the north by Highway 18, and on the south by Highway 60 and Interstate 10. This area also includes the Cajon and San Gorgonio Passes through which much air traffic enters and leaves the Greater Los Angeles Basin.

1911. *Wright Flyer "Vin Fizz"* crash-landed due to high winds in low hills of San Gorgonio Pass. Pilot was not injured and the aircraft was removed.

2/23/30. *Fokker F-10A, Western Air Express* crashed NE of Lake Arrowhead during a winter storm, killing all three crew on board. Wreckage was not located for twelve days. Large amount of unmarked debris still remains at crash site on 6,730' Shay Mountain. This site is ripe for a serious museum-directed recovery and display.

10/3/34. *Fokker C-14 USAAC* crashed at the top of Cajon Summit in cloudy weather. Three died and three survived this accident. Wreck was removed by US Army.

Date unknown. *1930s vintage wreckage* is located on Painted Hill at east end of San Gorgonio Pass.

3/29/37. *Northrop A-17 USAAC* crashed near the City Creek Forest Service Station, killing both crewmen. Wreck is unmarked and overgrown close to Highway 30. Weather was a factor in this accident.

1938-39. *Waco open cockpit biplane* crashed in bad weather near Cajon Pass summit and Highway 138. All three persons on board survived without serious injury. Wreck was removed

1939. *Travelaire NC-8842* crashed south of Lake Silverwood near Jobs Peak. No other data available.

1939. *Piper J-3 NC-22976* crashed in hills north of city of San Bernardino, killing both men on board. Pilot had been stunt flying. Wreck is removed.

6/9/41. *AT-6 or BT-13 USAAC* trainer crashed five miles north of Banning, killing one man and injuring another. Wreck is unmarked, but visible from the air.

10/13/41. *Douglas B-23 USAAF* crashed on the north side of the San Gorgonio Pass, killing all five men on board. Heavy winds were a factor in this accident. Wreck removed.

1941. *Douglas C-47 USAAC* hit ridge SW of Silverwood Lake east of Cajon Pass, killing all on board. This aircraft was carrying US Army payroll and therefore received special attention regarding wreckage clean-up. Only small unmarked parts remain at the site today.

1/2/42. *Martin B-26 #40-1475 USAAF* hit Keller Peak in bad weather, killing all nine men on board. This aircraft was enroute to March Field in Riverside County when the crash occurred. It was being sent to reinforce the Hawaiian Islands following the 12/7/41 attack by Japan. Today the R-2800 engines and landing gear struts are all that remain at this easy-to-reach site on the north slope just below the summit.

(For further details on 1/2/42 crash please see inset MAP next page)

1940s. *Vultee BT-13 USAAF* reported on north slope of Sugarloaf Mountain east of Big Bear Lake. This site is supposed to be marked but location and status have not been confirmed.

3/6/43. *Consolidated B-24H #42-52122 USAAF* hit Sugarpine Mountain east of Cajon Pass, killing all five men on board. Wreck is scattered and unmarked NE of town of Devore in timber.

6/5/43. *Consolidated B-24E USAAF* hit Painted Hill at the east end of San Gorgonio Pass and exploded, killing all on board. Small unmarked parts remain at site today.

1944-45. *North American SNJ-5 US Navy trainer* crashed on the south slope of Moon Ridge. Both crewman survived and one walked into Big Bear Lake for assistance. This site is marked and visible today. Weather was a factor in this accident.

Date unknown. *Lockheed P-38 USAAF* crashed north of community of Highland and west of Highway 30 at Mud Flat. Wreck was mostly removed

1/2/42. *Martin B-26 #40-1475 USAAF* crash site in the San Bernardino Mountains on Keller Peak. Take State Highway 330 to Running Springs then proceed east on Highway 18 towards Big Bear Lake taking 1N96 at the Deer Lick Station turn off. Follow 1N96 to the top of Keller Peak (7,882'). Most of this plane was removed in the 1950s.

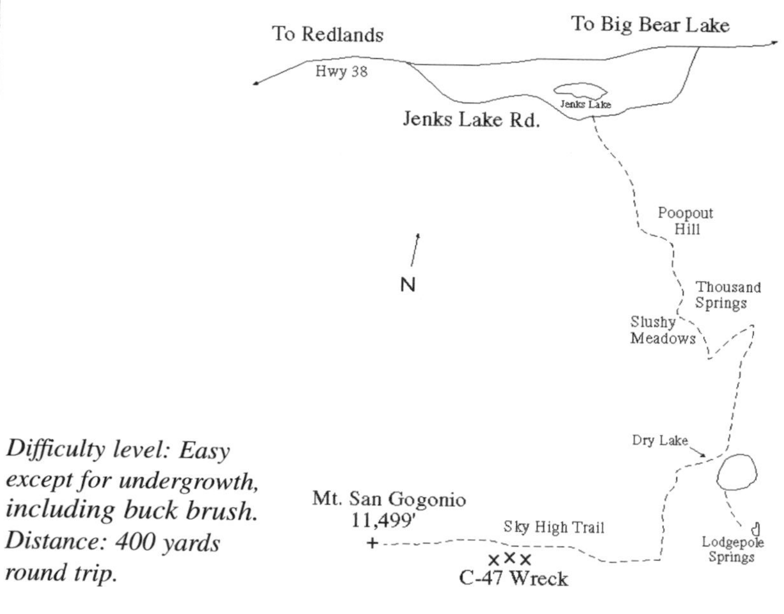

and covered. Site is near City Creek Forest Service Station.

1/16/44. *Vultee BT-13A USAAC training aircraft* crashed into Lake Arrowhead, killing both men on board. Site is in 30' of water near Totem Pole Point.

9/18/44. A *Military trainer* hit a mountain near Forest Home and the pilot survived. Status of wreck unknown today.

Date unknown. *Consolidated B-24 USAAF* crashed east of Big Bear Lake near Baldwin Lake. Wreckage is reported widely scattered and mostly removed.

1940s. *Vultee BT-13* crashed near Arrowhead Peak and is marked. Parts remain at site today.

1/21/45. *North American P-51D USAAF* crashed in Little Horse Thief Canyon, killing the pilot. Wreck is unmarked. Site is half mile east of Cajon Pass summit station.

1/22/45. *Lockheed P-38L USAAF* hit power lines near summit of Cajon Pass. The pilot died in the crash at Keenbrook Railroad mile post. Wreck is removed.

1945. *Stearman PT-17 USAAF* crashed in upper Fish Creek Meadows while on training flight. Both crewmen escaped serious injury and walked more than five miles to reach assistance. For many years this wreck was unmarked and visible until its removal in the late '60s. However, some parts are still reported at site, including the wings.

8/5/45. *US Navy plane* crashed while stunting near Clark's Ranch in the Santa Ana River Canyon. The pilot was killed and the site was bulldozed.

3/5/46. *Lightplane* crashed on Ketching Peak north of San Gorgonio Pass in bad weather. The pilot was killed and the wreck is unmarked.

Date unknown. *Taylorcraft* hit ridge east of Keller Peak. Site was marked but is no longer visible.

Date unknown. *Beachcraft Bonanza* crashed south of Mt. San Gorgonio on Morongo Indian Reservation, killing the pilot. This site is visible and marked.

Date unknown. *Fairchild PT-19 NC-56575* hit a mountain north of Banning while on a Civil Air Patrol search mission. The wreck is marked but is now overgrown by chaparral.

1950-51. *Cessna UC-78* crashed in mountains NE of Banning, killing all four men on board. Crash occurred in bad weather. Site is unmarked and status today is unknown.

Date unknown. *Vultee BT-13* crashed NW of Redlands after being stolen from an area airport. This site is marked and is located near Mt. Harrison.

11/28/52. *Douglas C-47B #45-1124 USAF* transport hit the east slope of Mt. San Gorgonio at 11,000' level. Thirteen Air Force personnel died in this accident that occurred in a blinding snowstorm. An Air Force helicopter crashed near the C-47 wreck without serious injury to its crew of two during rescue operations. This wreck was the first mountain crash site that I visited.

It was 1963 and, at that time, parachutes and personal effects littered the crash area. Since then a trail has been cut through the area and people have carried much material off the mountain. Large yellow X's mark this very visible site.

(For further details on 11/28/52 crash please see inset MAP below)

11/28/52. *Douglas C-47B #45-1124 USAF* east side of 11,499' Mt. San Gorgonio in the San Bernardino Mountains. This is a tough trip, but it's all there if you plan and execute an expedition-quality venture. Start by obtaining a San Gorgonio Wilderness entry and camping permit via Jenks Lake trail head to Poopout Hill, Slushy Meadows, Dry Lake or Lodgepole Spring for overnight camping. Plan on one day to reach base camp at either Dry Lake or Lodgepole Spring. Day Two requires an early start up the Sky High Trail towards the summit of Mt. San Gorgonio, also known as Greyback to locals. About two hours out of camp you will reach the lower, now widely scattered wreckage, of the C-47B. Fuselage, tail, wings, and engines are located between the 10,200' level and 11,000' level. Some hikers go on to the summit then retreat to camp and hike out the same day, reaching their cars between 6 pm and 7 pm.

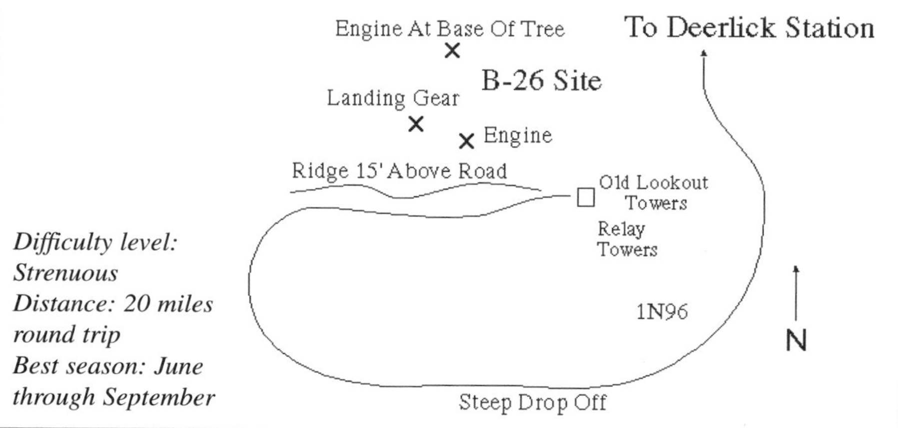

Difficulty level: Strenuous
Distance: 20 miles round trip
Best season: June through September

3/25/54. *Lightplane* crashed in Cajon Pass, killing three persons on board. No other information available.

1955. *Beechcraft SNB-5 US Navy* hit Cajon Mountain just below fire lookout, killing all on board. Although burned, the tail is still intact and marked. Bad weather was a factor in this crash.

1955. *North American TB-25J #44-86805 USAF* crashed south of Mt. San

Gorgonio at about the 8,900' level during bad weather. All on board were killed. Wreck is visible and marked.

Date unknown. *North American AT-6D #42-8569 USAF* crashed while on flight from Norton AFB. Pilot ran out of gas and was killed attempting to bail out NW of Big Bear Lake near Cienega Redondo. Wreck was missing for three months and, although it was marked, it may now be removed.

Date unknown. *Douglas Skyraider US Navy* crashed north of Holcomb Valley, killing the pilot. Aircraft flying up a canyon failed to clear ridge. Wreckage remains near John Bull Flat but is unmarked.

9/21/56. *North American F-100C #54-2027 USAF* crashed north of Patton following systems malfunction. The pilot safely ejected from the stricken plane. Wreck site is burned but marked parts are visible.

10/24/56. *North American F-86D #53-588 USAF* crashed and burned in Telephone Canyon south of Hesperia following pilot ejection. Wreckage is scattered and unmarked.

3/2/57. *Cessna 170 N1391D* disappeared on a flight from Los Angeles International Airport to Imperial, California. An extensive search at the time of the disappearance failed to locate any trace of N1391D. On 10/20/73 a Civil Air Patrol plane on a search mission for another missing aircraft located N1391D. The remains of all four persons were found at the remote site on a ridge above Mission Creek. Ironically, N1391D was located only 1,000' from a Mooney Mk. 20E that crashed on 5/7/71. The burned and scattered wreckage is unmarked and difficult to reach.

1/18/58. *Piper Tri-Pacer NC883A* hit Chaparosa Peak at 5,700' level, killing all four persons on board. Weather was a factor in this accident. Wreck is unmarked and difficult to see.

3/12/58. *Cessna C-172 N6870A* crashed on Arrowhead Peak killing four people. Site is north of Arrowhead Springs and is visible.

3/16/58. *Cessna 180 N9238C* crashed into Mt. San Gorgonio at the 8,000' level in bad weather, killing both persons on board. This wreck has been removed.

7/9/59. *Grumman TBM N9830C* crashed in Crafton Hills while on a fire-fighting mission. Pilot was killed and only a few parts remain at the site.

3/10/62. *Piper Cherokee N5315W* crashed in mountains three miles north of Banning in bad weather, killing all four people on board. Wreck is unmarked and mostly removed.

9/7/62. *Piper Cherokee N9358W* crashed shortly after taking off from Big Bear Lake Airport with a family of four on board. Crash site is in Red Ant Canyon on the south slope of Moon Ridge, only a half mile from cabins. Yet the wreck was undiscovered for several days. Interestingly, the crash site was found by the grandfather the family had been visiting in Big Bear. While both adults riding in the front seat died, two children in the back seat survived. This accident occurred in clear weather with density, altitude, and pilot error as factors. Wreck is unmarked and only a few parts remain.

3/7/64. *Cessna 172 N7778T* vanished in bad weather with two persons on board. Wreck was discovered by a woodcutter on 4/7/64 in Lightning Gulch near Onyx Summit at 8,400' level. Wreck has been removed.

5/19/64. *Stinson 10A* force landed in Holcomb Valley without injury to the only man on board. Aircraft was removed.

The author and tubular fuselage structure of a North American Aviation SNJ-5 US Navy that crashed south of Big Bear Lake in 1944-45. Both Crewman escaped with minor injuries. (P. J. Macha) Region 6.

U.S. Navy TA-4J

Landing gear leg of US Navy TA-4J in upper Lovelace Canyon. (G.P. Macha) Region 6.

5/27/64. *North American F-100D USAF* crashed below Running Springs, killing the pilot. Wreckage is scattered and burned. Weather was a factor in this accident.

6/8/64. *Beechcraft Travelaire N2055C* crashed into cloud-enshrouded San Bernardino Peak at 7,300' level, killing all three people on board. While weather was a factor in this crash, the pilot misheard ground control giving a new heading to another aircraft and followed that heading with tragic consequences. This site is burned, partly covered, and unmarked.

Date unknown. *Fairchild PT-23* crashed 1.4 miles west of Arrowhead Springs Hotel after running out of fuel. One person was injured, one killed in the crash. Wreck was removed.

4/8/66. *Sikorsky H-34 US Navy* lost power and crashed on the south slope of

Moon Ridge near Big Bear Lake. No one was hurt and the H-34 was removed, repaired, and returned to service.

10/11/66. *Mooney Mk. 21 N6969U* crashed below Crestline in Waterman Canyon while flying in cloudy weather. Wreck is marked. Casualties not known.

11/7/66. *Cessna 172* hit ridge in Cajon Pass in bad weather. Both persons on board survived with minor injuries. Wreck has been removed.

4/1/67. *Piper Twin Comanche N7979Y* crashed at 4,700' level of Cajon Pass, killing two and injuring one. Weather was a factor in crash and wreckage has been removed.

4/28/67. *Piper Cherokee N6361R* crashed in bad weather at Crab Flats near Green Valley, killing all four persons on board. This site was marked but may now be removed.

8/9/67. *Piper Apache N2228P* crashed in cloudy weather in low hills near Yucaipa, killing both persons on board. Wreckage was removed.

6/8/68. *Cessna 172 N4140L* hit Dobbs Peak at 9,800' level, killing the four people on board. Crash occurred at night. Wreck is marked.

2/28/69. *Piper Cherokee N7157R* crashed, killing one man in bad weather near mountain community of Blue Jay. Wreck has been removed.

5/3/69. *Lightplane* crashed on Cajon Summit in cloudy weather. All four persons escaped without injury and wreck was removed.

5/17/69. *Cessna 172 N4503L* crashed at night near Baldwin Dry Lake east of Big Bear Lake. Aircraft ran out of gas while pilot was on joy ride. All three on board perished in crash. Wreck has been removed.

10/17/69. *Cessna Skymaster N1234V* hit Ketching Peak at 5,400' level, killing five people on board. Weather was a factor in the crash and wreckage is still visible.

11/10/69. *Cessna 182C N8916T* hit mountain peak west of Big Bear Lake, killing both persons. Weather was a factor in crash. Parts visible at site.

2/10/70. *Mooney Mk. 21 N2715W* hit a 5,500' peak north of Banning, killing the pilot in another weather-related accident.

3/4/70. *Piper Cherokee 235 N9128W* crashed one mile south of Cajon Summit and burned, killing four persons on board. Weather was a factor in this crash. Wreck has been removed.

1970. Douglas TA-4J USN crashed in upper Lovelace Canyon SE of Apple Valley. Wreck is white, orange, and scattered. Aircraft had been assigned to VA-124 at Miramar NAS.

11/28/70. *Cessna 150* crashed three miles north of Devore Heights in Cajon Pass, killing the only person on board. Weather was a factor in this crash.

11/28/70. *Globe Swift* crashed near Running Springs, killing the pilot. Accident occurred in bad weather. Wreck has been removed.

12/1/70. *Bell 47* crashed in mountains west of Running Springs, killing the pilot. Weather was a factor in this crash. Wreck has been removed.

2/2/71. *Piper Tri-Pacer* crashed 1/4 mile east of Interstate 15 in Cajon Pass, killing all three on board. Wreckage is burned and mostly removed.

2/21/71. *Cessna 177* crashed on ridge north of Big Bear Lake, killing three and seriously injuring one. Wreckage is mostly removed.

4/19/71. *Piper Cherokee* crashed in rugged White Water Canyon within the boundaries of San Gorgonio Wilderness. Four persons were killed in this accident that was weather-related. Wreckage is marked and visible.

4/26/71. *Cessna 172* crashed at 5,000' level of Devil's Canyon near Panorama Point. All three persons on board survived with only minor injuries.

5/7/71. *Mooney Mk. 20E* carrying three persons hit trees at top of ridge and plunged into a steep canyon with fatal results. This site is marked and is located east of Heart Bar State Park in the uppermost end of the north fork of Mission Creek.

9/5/71. *Cessna 172* crashed on Highway 38 near Heart Bar State Park, killing one person and seriously injuring another in what investigators described as a pilot error accident. Wreckage completely removed.

11/24/71. *Cessna 172 N3715P* crashed east of Big Bear Lake, killing the only person on board. Weather was a factor in this accident. Status of wreck is not known.

12/22/71. *Lightplane* crashed east of Big Bear Lake in bad weather and the only person on board escaped injury. Wreck was removed.

1/26/72. *American Yankee* crashed in Devil's Canyon, killing the pilot. Site is east of Cajon Pass and is mostly removed. Accident was weather-related.

11/5/72. *Cessna 140* hit Rebel Ridge and burned, killing both persons on board. Wreckage is removed.

6/14/73. *Piper PA-28 N4806L* hit Snow Peak at 6,500' level, killing the pilot. Site is located north of Banning and parts are visible. Weather related accident.

1/7/74. *Beechcraft Baron* crashed four miles south of Big Bear at 8,000' level of Moon Ridge. All three persons on board were killed and scattered wreckage remains visible at site today.

3/23/74. *Cessna 180 N4808Z* crashed in mountains north of Banning. Other data not known.

Date unknown. *Beechcraft Debonair* crashed north of Morongo Valley in

Piper Cherokee N9358W

Piper Cherokee crashed at Moonridge south of Big Bear Lake on 9/7/62. Two adults died but two children survived for two days and were saved. (NTSB) Region 6.

the San Bernardino Mountains. No other data available on this crash.

9/8/74. *Piper Comanche* crashed in mountains eight miles NE of Lake Arrowhead, causing serious injury to one person and minor injury to another.

2/14/75. *Beechcraft Bonanza* crashed at 3,700' level NW of Banning, killing the only person on board. Accident was weather-related.

5/23/75. *Cessna 310 N5481A* hit ridge east of Mission Creek at 8,000' level at night. Four persons died and one survived. Wreck is mostly removed.

6/7/75. *Beechcraft N2055C* crashed near Mountain Home Village east of Highway 38. Wreck is marked.

11/28/75. *Beechcraft Bonanza N1528Z* crashed on north rim of Holcomb Valley in bad weather, killing all three on board. Wreck is mostly removed, but parts do remain at the site near old mining digs.

2/7/76. *Cessna 182 N6716M* crashed on Sugarloaf Mountain in bad weather. All four persons on board escaped injury. Intact wreck was removed.

2/15/76. *Beechcraft Bonanza* hit mountainside 1/4 mile south of Crestline Junction in bad weather, killing the pilot. Wreck removed.

2/14/76. Bellanca 230 N9816B disappeared on a flight from Santa Barbara to Guaymas, Mexico, with four people on board. An extensive air search failed to locate the missing plane. On 7/29/76 the wreckage was spotted at 9,500' level east of San Bernardino Peak and south of Barton Flats. Wreckage is smashed, unmarked, and has not been removed.

3/17/76. *Beechcraft Bonanza* hit Galena Peak in bad weather, killing the pilot. Wreck has been removed.

9/22/76. A *Sikorsky S-55* on a medical emergency flight crashed in fog shrouded Cajon Pass, killing all four on board. Crash site was near Cleghorn Road. Wreck has been removed.

10/2/76. *Piper PA-28* crashed near a youth camp SE of Sugarloaf Mountain. Both persons on board escaped injury in this weather-related accident. Wreck is removed.

1/6/77. *Gates-Lear Jet N12MK* crashed at 9,500' level of Ten Thousand Foot Ridge after taking off from Palm Springs. All four persons on board died in crash, including Frank Sinatra's mother. Scattered wreckage remains visible at this site today. Pilot error has been listed as the cause of this crash.

2/21/77. *Beechcraft Bonanza* crashed in bad weather 1/2 mile south of Snow Summit ski lifts, killing all four persons on board. Wreckage has been removed.

4/1/77. *Cessna 411 N9100V* crashed in bad weather at Crab Flats near Green Valley Lake. All seven persons on board were killed. Wreck is removed.

8/8/77. *Cessna 172* crashed in bottom of Bear Creek, west of Big Bear Lake Dam, killing both persons on board. This wreck is visible and unmarked.

1/4/78. *Piper Tri-Pacer* crashed in bad weather in Cleghorn Canyon of Cajon Pass, killing all three people on board. Wreck has been removed.

7/31/78. *Cessna 172* crashed at 9,500' level near Dollar Lake in the San Gorgonio Wilderness. One person died and three survived with serious injuries. Pilot error was listed as the primary cause in this crash.

Jeff Boal and propellor of Douglas C-47B #45-1124 at 11,300 level of Mt. San Gorgonio. (G.P. Macha) Region 6.

AT-6D
#42-8569 USAF

The unmarked wreck of an AT-6D crashed killing the pilot NW of Big Bear Lake near Cienega Redondo sometime in 1953. (B.F. Giebeler) Region 6.

4/16/79. *Cessna 170 N2509C* hit east slope of Onyx Peak, killing all three people on board. Status of wreck is not known.

6/8/79. A *Fairchild C-119* crashed on fire-fighting mission in Millard Canyon north of Banning. Both crewmen were killed and structural failure is suspected as a cause of this crash. Wreck is burned and partly removed.

8/20/79. *Piper Twin Comanche N8139A* hit hills NE of Redlands in heavy fog, killing both persons on board. Wreck is removed.

4/11/80. *Lightplane* crashed in hills east of Redlands, killing two persons. Weather was a factor in this accident.

7/17/80. *Boeing-Vertol CH-47 US Army* crashed and burned south of Highway 38 near Heart Bar State Park. One man died and three survived this accident. Only a few parts remain at this site.

10/15/80. *Piper PA-28 N2212D* crashed east of Cajon Pass on Cajon Mountain. Status of wreck is unknown.

1/21/81. *Lightplane* hit ridge north of Banning in bad weather, killing two people.

4/18/81. *Mooney Mk. 21* hit ridge north of Banning at 2,300' level in bad weather, killing the pilot.

5/30/81. *Sikorsky S-55 N874* hit mountain ridge near Beaumont, killing all six persons on board. Helicopter was on medical emergency flight. Weather was cloudy/foggy at time of crash.

7/3/81. *Beechcraft Bonanza* crashed near Baldwin Dry Lake, east of Big Bear Lake, killing the pilot. Wreck is removed.

1/22/82. *Beechcraft Baron N3995Q* lies wrecked NW of Banning in San Bernardino Mountains.

5/1/83. *Piper Warrior N9233K* crashed at bottom of Bear Creek Canyon, NE of Redlands, killing all four persons on board. Wreckage is visible.

12/28/84. *Cessna 182 N5948J* hit ridge above Siberia Creek, killing all five people on board. Plane had just taken off from Big Bear Lake Airport and entered haze layer. Pilot error is a factor in this crash. Wreckage partly removed.

11/27/85. *Cessna 177* crashed four miles NE of Highland in the San Bernardino Mountains, killing all four persons on board. Bad weather was a factor in crash.

8/7/86. *Cessna* crashed in rugged Mission Creek, but both people on board escaped injury. Status of wreck is unknown.

2/23/87. *Cessna 206* crashed NE of Lake Arrowhead and burned, killing both people on board. Weather was a factor in this accident.

3/21/87. *McDonnell Douglas F-4C California Air National Guard* crashed at 5,500' level north of Banning in cloudy weather. Both airmen were killed and some wreckage is still visible at site. Actor Dean Martin's son was the pilot.

4/16/87. *Helicopter* crash-landed at 5,800' level of Little San Gorgonio Peak. All three on board escaped injury and wreck was removed.

5/17/88. *Aerospatiale Twinstar* hit power lines after picking up an accident victim on Interstate 15 in Cajon Pass north of Devore. Highway accident victim survived the crash but the pilot and nurse did not. Wreck was removed.

8/24/89. *Rockwell International OV-10A USMC #155485* disappeared on this date with two men on board. Wreck was located 9/9/89 by Civil Air

Patrol search aircraft. The crash site is located SE of Mt. San Gorgonio summit in the rugged White Water River Canyon at 6,100' level. The bodies of both crewmen were found at the impact point. Sadly, they ejected too late. Wreckage is scattered on a near vertical face and is unmarked. Weather was clear at time of crash.

1/5/89. *Piper PA-28 N5157L* crashed south of Cajon Mountain north of Devore. Wreck is reported removed.

9/17/89. *Cessna 310* crashed in cloudy weather south of Hesperia on the north slope of the San Bernardino Mountains, SE of Interstate 15, at the entrance to Cajon Pass. Two people perished in this accident. Wreckage is burned and mostly removed.

3/2/91. *Beechcraft BE-58 N66660* crashed near Siberia Creek SW of Big Bear Lake. Status of wreck is unknown.

9/13/91. *Cessna 210 N6558X* crashed in mountains near Devore. Wreck is reported removed.

11/14/91. *Cessna 336 Skymaster N3848U* crashed in bad weather on the north slope of the San Bernardino Mountains near 7,740' White Mountain, killing all five persons on board. The plane had been enroute from Bullhead City, Arizona, to Fullerton Municipal Airport when it disappeared. The wreck of N3848U was finally discovered by a helicopter hired by relatives of the missing pilot and passengers on 7/5/92. The heavy winter snowpack had hampered search efforts that did result, however, in locating a Mooney Mk. missing since 8/5/83 on the Mojave Desert. Unmarked parts are still reported as visible today at the crash site.

2/16/92. *Piper PA-31 N60AW* crashed SW of Big Bear Lake at the 7,000' level the Santa Ana River Canyon. All seven persons aboard died in this weather-related accident. The aircraft had been enroute from Tijuana, Mexico, to Big Bear Lake Airport. Wreck is reported removed.

3/15/92. *Lightplane* crashed west of Highway 38 near community of Angelus Oaks. All three persons on board survived. Status of wreck is unknown.

6/95. *McDonnell Douglas 500D helicopter* crashed in mountains near Mentone Dam construction site. All four on board survived. Wreck was removed.

REGION 7

Region 7 includes all of the San Gabriel Mountains and all of the Angeles National Forest, as well as a portion of the San Bernardino National Forest. The highest peak in this area is 10,064' Mt. San Antonio, also known as Mt. Baldy. The eastern boundary of this region is Interstate 15 and Highway 138 on the north. Western and southern boundaries are Interstates 5, 210, and Highway 66. In this vast area north and east of metropolitan Los Angeles, more than 225 aircraft have crashed. The topography of this region includes alpine forests, chaparral brush lands, barren desert, and fire-blackened mountain slopes. Region 7, while close to a huge urban population, also contains the remnants of several long-missing airplanes. Region 7 is also the location of the first aviation accident in the history of the American West.

1909. *Sightseeing balloon* carrying paying customers from Pasadena drifted into snow-covered Strawberry Peak. The pilot and passengers walked to Colby's Ranch for assistance. The gondola was seen on the mountainside for many years but no trace remains today.

10/26/27. *Ryan M-1 of Pacific Air Transport* crashed and burned NE of Castaic, following pilot bail-out in bad weather.

2/2/32. *Lightplane* crashed in bad weather north of San Fernando in foothills. The pilot escaped injury.

11/15/35. *Northrop Alpha of TWA* crashed on mail flight near Newhall in hills. Pilot was injured and wreck was removed.

11/16/35. *Travelaire 6000* hit hillside near Newhall in rainstorm, killing all four persons on board. Wreckage is smashed and mostly removed.

Date unknown. *Curtiss Robin* lies burned and unmarked near San Sevaine Flats north of Fontana. No other data available.

1936. *Boeing P-12E USAAC* crashed in bad weather west of San Sevaine Peak and north of Fontana. The pilot was killed and most of the wreck has been salvaged.

1/12/37. *Boeing 247D NC-13306 of Western Air Express* crashed into the north slope of Pinetos Peak near San Fernando. One crew member and four passengers died in the crash. However, two ot the crew and six passengers survived with serious injuries. The well-known African explorer Martin Johnson died in the crash but his wife, Osa, survived. This was a weather-related accident. Only a few small parts remain at site today.

5/18/38. Lockheed Super Electra Model 14H c/n 1439, NC-17394 of Northwest Airlines hit Stroh Peak 1.5 miles north of Mint Canyon Road, killing all nine on board. Bad weather was a factor in this crash. Wreck is mostly removed from its 2,200' impact site.

1941. *Piper Cub* crashed on Granite Peak east of Mt. Gleason, killing both people on board.

6/23/41. *North American AT-6* crashed in a spur of Eaton Canyon north of Pasadena in bad weather, killing the pilot. Aircraft was being delivered to Canada. Wreck is unmarked and burned in rugged Rubio Canyon.

9/20/42. *Vultee BT-13A USAAF trainer* hit Table Mountain near Wrightwood and burned. Both crewmen perished in crash. Wreck is removed.

Curtis C-46A #41-12363 USAAF hit north slope of Pallet Mtn. on 2/25/44 during a snowstorm. All four crewman died in the crash. (S. Griggers Circa 1944) Region 7.

10/26/42. *Lightplane* crashed near Camp Baldy in brush-covered canyon, injuring both men on board. One source indicates aircraft was military observation type. Wreck was removed.

1943. *Douglas SBD-3 USN* is located on the NW slope of Magic Mountain above Spring Canyon. Wreckage is blue, scattered, and visible. Reaching this site without a helicopter is very difficult, due to heavy chaparral ground cover.

4/7/43. *Vultee BT-13 USAAF* is 350' below summit of Mt. Lukens on north slope. Wreck was discovered by a deer hunter on 12/12/43. The body of a US Army Major was removed the next day. This site is unmarked and extremely difficult to see because of the dense undergrowth.

2/25/44. *Curtiss C-46A #41-12363 of USAAF* hit Pallet Mountain during a winter storm, killing all four crewmen. Site is marked and highly-visible on the north slope of the mountain above Devil's Punch Bowl County Park. On 10/3/66 a *USAF C-119* crashed 200 yards above the *C-46*.

2/25/44. *Lockheed PV-1 US Navy* on test flight from Burbank to Palmdale, with four-man company flight test crew on board, crashed on Sierra Pelona Ridge nine miles north of Acton Junction. All four men were killed in this weather-related accident. Wreck was bulldozed over at the 5,000' level on the south slope of the ridge. The wife of air pilot had a memorial plaque placed at the crash site. The partial excavation of this wreck was started in 1996.

3/24/44. *Lockheed P-38 USAAF* crashed south of the town of Littlerock, killing the pilot. This site has been partly salvaged by helicopter, but is still visible at 4,600' level of Cooper Canyon.

6/20/44. *Vultee BT-13 USAAF* crashed in Icehouse Canyon north of Mt. Baldy village. Pilot is said to have survived and the intact wreck was partly removed. Recent attempts to locate this site have not been successful.

7/6/44. *Lockheed P-38L USAAF* crashed in San Gabriel Mountains near Junction of Kagel and Lopez Canyons. Pilot died in crash. Only small parts remain at site today.

Date unknown. *Consolidated B-24 USAAF* crashed in rugged middle fork of Lytle Creek west of ranger station. Wreck was marked with black X's but is no longer visible and may be overgrown. 34° 13'N Lat. 117° 33'W long.

Date unknown. *Lockheed P-38L USAAF* crashed near Sierra Highway and Ave. C., 600' from end of road. Many small unmarked parts remain.

9/28/44. *Lockheed P-38L USAAF* hit ridge south of Mt. Wilson, killing the pilot. Wreck was marked but later salvaged. Parts remain on Mt. Yale impact site.

10/6/44. *Curtiss C-46 USAAF* crashed near South Mt. Hawkins at about 6,000' level. Wreck is not marked, is overgrown, and hard to see. Entire crew perished in this weather-related crash.

11/7/44. *Lockheed P-38L #44-24918 USAAF* crashed and burned on test flight from Burbank Airport, killing the pilot. Some unmarked wreckage remains visible in upper reaches of Little Tujunga Canyon.

1944. *Lockheed P-38L USAAF* hit slope Mt. McDill west of Palmdale. Status of wreck unknown.

11/13/44. *Douglas C-47B #43-16143 USAAF* crashed in Wildcat Gulch on the north side of Barley Flats. Heavy clouds blanketed the San Gabriel Mountains at time of accident. Several US Army passengers survived for a number of hours following impact but died after rescuers arrived. Only one of the thirteen men on board recovered from his injuries. This site is marked with yellow X's and is now badly scattered over several miles in lower Wildcat Gulch.

12/24/44. *Consolidated B-24 USAAF* crashed in a storm on south slope of Mt. Gleason, killing all ten men on board. This site is marked and scattered for 3.5 miles in Mill Creek drainage. Substantial salvage work has been done on this wreck.

12/25/44. *Vultee BT-13B #42-90434 USAAF* crashed while circling B-24 wreck. The pilot survived and the intact BT was marked. Today only a few parts remain of this wreck. See 3/10/51 for related accident.

3/15/45. *Taylorcraft NC-24493* hit Vetter Peak in cloudy weather without injury to pilot. Wreck was removed.

3/19/45. *Grumman FM-2 USN* crashed in Newhall Pass east of Interstate 5 following in-flight fire and pilot bailout. Wreck is removed.

4/19/45. *Lockheed P-38L USAAF* hit ridge one mile east of Mt. McDill, killing the pilot. Scattered unmarked parts remain at site.

10/5/45. *C-46A #41-5190 USAAF* hit summit of Mt. San Antonio in bad weather, killing the entire crew. Most of the wreckage went over the north side of the mountain and lies unmarked and extremely difficult to reach on a nearly vertical face. Some debris is visible on the summit of west peak while stabilizer section is situated on south slope at 9,700' level.

7/2/47. *North American AT-6C #42-48918* of the California National Guard crashed in rugged Grand Canyon west of Mt. Lowe. Crash occurred in bad weather, killing the pilot. Some salvage work was completed but one wing with original markings is still there. Wreck is not easily visible from the air and is located close to canyon bottom.

Date unknown. *Douglas C-47 USAAF* crashed at 6,000' level above the middle fork of Lytle Creek. Wreck was marked and visible for many years, but is no longer reported today.

10/24/47. *Douglas A-26C USAF* hit Cucamonga Peak at 6,000' level on south slope, killing all five men on board. Crash occurred in bad weather. The wreck is marked and was visible for many years but may have been recently salvaged. Wreck was in Day Canyon.

Date unknown. *Gruman TBM US Navy* is reported wrecked south of Palmdale near Kentucky Springs. No other data available.

Date unknown. *Cessna NC-76493* is located west of Lytle Creek in rugged terrain. Site is marked and overgrown at 7,200' level.

Date unknown. *North American SNJ-6 #112349 US Navy* crashed near summit of Monrovia Peak. Site is marked and was highly visible until a series of brush and timber fires ravaged the area.

Date unknown. *Lockheed F-80C USAF* crashed on the north slope of Circle Mountain east of town of Wrightwood. Unmarked wing visible in mid-1970s.

5/7/48. *Noorduyn Norseman NC-54231* crashed 1/4 mile east of Brown Mountain in a small saddle. Both men on board survived with minor injuries. This wreck is not marked, but very interesting to visit because of all the aircraft parts that remain. I examined this wreck in 1968 and found that all of the manufacturer's identification plates were completely blank.

10/28/48. *Vultee BT-13 NC-67869* crashed in Dunsmore Canyon south of Mt. Lukens, killing the pilot on board. The weather was a factor in this crash. This site is unmarked and burned over by several area brush fires.

3/6/49. Two *Grumman F6F-5 USMC Hellcats* hit Mt. San Antonio at 9,500' level on south slope in snowstorm. Both pilots were killed in this "formation" accident. Neither aircraft burned and are now often visited by persons seeking parts to assist in F6F restoration projects. Although marked, these wrecks are hard to see from the air since their blue paint schemes blend in with rock and alpine ground cover. Wrecks are about 100 yards apart and squadron markings are still visible. Both aircraft were based at USMAS El Toro.

7/23/49. *Aeronca* hit north slope of Magic Mountain in Pole Canyon near Douglas SBD crash site. Both men on board survived this pilot error mishap. Wreck was marked but is no longer visible.

Curtiss C-46A
#41-12363

Wreckage of tail section of a Curtiss C-46A. (P.J. Macha) Region 7.

9/21/49. *North American F-51D #44-73080 California Air National Guard* hit ridge 1.5 miles SE junction of Gold Creek and Little Tujunga Canyons, killing the pilot. Site was bulldozed over, only a few small parts are visible.

Date unknown. *Lightplane* crashed north of San Dimas in heavy chaparral. Wreck is unmarked.

4/22/50. *Ryan Navion N3109K* hit Pine Mountain east of Monrovia Peak. Wreck is unmarked and burned over.

9/27/50. *Cessna 170 N9049A* hit Will Thrall Peak, killing both people on board. Accident occurred in cloudy weather. I have not been able to locate this site, but it is still reported visible as of 9/90.

2/14/51. *North American Navion NC-5674X* crashed in Chimney Canyon west of Mt. Gleason in bad weather. The pilot died in this accident and wreck was marked.

3/10/51. *Cessna 140* crashed while circling wrecks of B-24 and BT-13 on Mt. Gleason. Both Civil Air Patrol men on board were killed in this pilot error accident. Wreck is unmarked and visible at bottom of steep canyon.

4/6/51. *Howard DGA-16-8 NG67765* wreck is located on Mt. McDill south of Quartz Hill, at top of Willow Springs Canyon. Site is burned and difficult to see, but fuselage and engine are visible.

1/27/52. *Piper J-3 N3637N* crashed in Big Tujunga Canyon without injury to pilot. Wreck was removed.

3/4/52. *Fletcher FD-25 Defender NX90609* crashed in Pacoima Canyon while on test flight, killing both crewmen. Wreck was removed.

5/28/52. *Lockheed F-5G N67864* crashed and burned in Sand Canyon west of Magic Mountain, killing the pilot. This site is unmarked and parts are still visible. Pilot error was listed as the cause of this accident.

6/8/52. *Douglas C-47 USAF* hit east slope of Mt. Wilson at 3,200' level, killing all seven men on board. Crash occurred in cloudy weather. Site is marked and overgrown.

11/21/52. *Luscombe 8E N1912K* hit Mt. Harvard above Pasadena in bad weather, killing the pilot. Site is unmarked and burned over.

1953. *Bell 47* hit ridge west of Baden-Powell, killing the pilot. Ridge is now called Copter Ridge as a memorial to the dead flyer. Scattered parts remain at site.

6/6/53. *Luscombe 8E N1542K* crashed in Bailey Canyon north of Sierra Madre, killing the pilot. Weather was a factor in this crash that remained unlocated until 3/26/54. Site is unmarked and overgrown.

3/24/54. *Beechcraft Staggerwing N65K* disappeared on a flight from Las Vegas to Los Angeles with four persons on board. Wreck was found by a hiker on 10/24/59 in upper Coldwater Canyon on north slope of Telegraph Peak. Wreck is unmarked and difficult to see.

4/18/54. *Aerocoupe* crashed 14 miles NE of Newhall near Solemint Junction. Both persons on board were seriously injured in this bad weather related accident. Wreck has been removed.

11/1/54. *Cessna 195 N4347* hit SE San Sevaine Peak in bad weather. Site is unmarked and mostly removed.

1/6/55. *North American F-51H #44-64368 California Air National Guard* crashed one mile south of Acton, killing the pilot. Wreck is removed.

6/29/56. *Cessna 120 N77120* crashed west of Big Pines in L.A. County while enroute from Big Bear Lake Airport. Wreck was not located until 7/22/56 with remains of the pilot and his two children. Status of this site is unknown.

9/4/56. Two *North American F-86A-Js #48-313 and #49-1338* of California Air National Guard collided over Mt.Pacifico while on a routine training mission. One pilot ejected and survived, while the other died. Both wrecks are scattered and burned with one tail and wing assembly still visible one half mile north of Loomis Ranch.

10/28/56. *Piper Tri-Pacer N7046B* disappeared with three people on board and was not located until 6/6/60 on the NE slope of Cucamonga Peak. Weather was a factor in this crash. Wreck is unmarked and very difficult to see.

2/2/57. *Grumman F9F-5 #195559 US Navy* hit ridge north of Mt. San Antonio in bad weather, killing the pilot. Wreck is scattered and unmarked at 8,000' level.

3/4/57. *Cessna 170* crashed in mountains 20 miles north of Newhall, killing both people on board. Accident occurred in bad weather. Wreckage has been removed.

7/22/58. *Champion Tri-Champ N9008B* was listed intact 1.5 miles SW of Pinetos Peak in canyon bottom. No other data available.

2/10/59. *Lockheed T-33A #56-3683 USAF* hit west slope of Mt. San Antonio at 9,500' level, killing both men on board. Aircraft was missing for several months due to heavy snowpack, but was finally located 6/17/59. Wreck is scattered and marked.

Date unknown. *Sikorsky H-19B #51-3441 USAF* crashed while on rescue mission. Site is located south of Vincent Gap near Mt. Baden-Powell. No one was killed in this accident and only the rotor blades remain unsalvaged today.

1958. Two *Luscombe aircraft* on Civil Air Patrol mission crashed on Cucamonga Peak. Two men perished and two survived in serious condition. These sites are unmarked and possibly removed.

2/15/59. Piper Tri-Pacer N1938D crashed in bad weather near Gorman. The pilot survived and wreck was removed.

2/20/59. *Taylorcraft L2A* crashed in Bouquet Canyon one half mile from reservoir. Pilot died in this weather-related crash. Wreck is unmarked.

4/29/59. *Aeronca 7AC N2403E* hit NW slope of Brown Mountain, killing the pilot. Site is unmarked and may be removed.

1/11/60. *Beechcraft Bonanza N7949D* hit power lines in bad weather, killing both persons on board. Crash site near Castaic Junction is burned and unmarked.

1/24/60. A *Taylorcraft N50855* hit Glendora Ridge, seriously injuring two persons. Wreck is unmarked and burned at the top of Little Dalton Canyon.

1/24/60. *Cessna 140 N89764* crashed three miles west of Lake Hughes, killing both men on board. Wreck is intact and unmarked. Weather was a factor in this accident.

5/14/60. *Lightplane* hit mountain eight miles NE of Fontana, killing the only person on board.

5/14/60. *North American T-6 N28016* hit Pinetos Peak, killing the pilot and his wife. Wreck was near road and is completely removed. Weather was a factor in this accident.

5/16/60. *Beechcraft Bonanza N7206B* disappeared enroute from Las Vegas to Los Angeles with four persons on board. Wreck was not located until 11/30/60 on north slope of Mt. Wilson. A forest ranger found the site that included the body of pianist Liberace's brother. Aircraft was lost in bad weather. Wreck is marked and was mostly removed in 1970s.

7/23/60. *North American B-25 N34466* crashed at bottom of Mill Canyon while on fire-fighting mission. Site is at 4,500' level unmarked and visible. Pilot died in crash.

9/23/60. *Lockheed F-104* (on loan to Navy) hit Josephine Peak at 4,500' level on south slope. Aircraft exploded and burned. The pilot died instantly in this weather-related accident. Site unmarked with few small fragments visible.

9/27/60. *Grumman TBM-3 N9598C* hit south slope of Brown Mountain at 3,200' level while on fire-fighting mission. Pilot died in this crash. Wreck is highly visible and unmarked.

11/30/61. *Homebuilt lightplane* crashed in Boy Scout Canyon above San Fernando, killing pilot. Wreck is removed.

Date unknown. *North American F-100 USAF* hit Mt. Baden-Powell and exploded. Scattered wreckage is visible on SE side of mountain.

11/30/61. *Beechcraft Travelaire N92MK* hit north slope of Pinetos Ridge, killing the pilot. Wreck is visible and marked at 3,500' level. Weather was a factor in this crash.

3/7/62. *Vultee BT-13 N57226* crashed in San Francisquito Canyon in bad weather, killing the pilot. Wreckage is removed.

9/19/63. *Ryan Navion* crashed near summit of Mt. Wilson in bad weather, killing pilot. Site is unmarked with few parts remaining.

2/23/64. *Stinson 108 N97244* crashed in mountains east of Newhall, seriously injuring both persons on board. Weather was a factor in this accident.

3/23/64. *Cessna 172 N5994A* crashed four miles east of Wrightwood in

Lone Pine Canyon. All four persons on board escaped without serious injury. Wreck is removed and crash was weather-related.

4/24/64. *Cessna 150 N615CF* hit Cucamonga Peak at 3,200' level, killing the pilot. Crash occurred in cloudy weather. Status of site is unknown.

12/19/64. *Beechcraft Model 50 N4931B* hit the near vertical face of ridge near Mt. Disappointment in bad weather, killing both persons on board. Wreck is marked and scattered at 5,300' level.

1/1/65. *Beechcraft T-34A Mentor N5506V* crashed six miles west of Wrightwood near Vincent Gap, killing both men on board. The wreck was located by a hiker on 7/31/65. The aircraft had impacted in a vertical dive in heavy woods and was very difficult to see. While weather was a factor in

North American Aviation B-25J N34466

North American Aviation B-25J crashed on fire-fighting mission on 7/23/60 in Mill Canyon near Mt. Gleason, killing the pilot. (P. J. Macha) Region 7.

this accident, pilot error was listed as the primary cause. Wreck is marked and has been partly salvaged.

2/18/65. *Cessna 182* suffered structural failure while flying in high winds two miles west of Big Pines. The aircraft crashed and burned, killing both persons on board. Wreck has been removed.

5/23/65. Cessna 172 N2597U hit San Sevaine Peak at 3,500' level in cloudy weather, killing both persons on board. Wreck is unmarked and mostly removed.

9/18/65. *Piper Cherokee N5871W* hit mountains north of Altadena at 3,000' level, killing both people on board. Wreck is marked. Crash occurred in cloudy weather.

3/31/66. *Cessna 172D N2958U* hit NW slope of Magic Mountain, killing the pilot. Site is burned and marked with black X's. Accident was weather-related.

9/30/66. *Fairchild C-119C USAF Reserve* aircraft hit summit of Pallet Mountain in stormy weather, killing the four-man crew. Wreck is marked and highly visible. This site is about 200 yards above the C-46 that crashed 2/25/44.

10/1/66. *Bell 47G-2 USFS* crashed enroute to C-119 accident site, injuring the three men on board. Some parts remain at the Islip Canyon crash site.

10/6/66. *Piper Cherokee N8682W* crashed on ridge above Day Canyon, killing the only person on board. Weather was a factor in this accident. Wreck is unmarked.

3/12/67. *Cessna 172 N3715R* hit mountains NE of Newhall in bad weather, killing two persons on board. Wreck is removed.

4/4/67. *Beechcraft Model 95 N117S* hit mountain ridge near Saugus in bad weather, killing two persons. Wreckage is mostly removed.

4/15/67. *Cessna 150 N4181U* hit mountain in Newhall Pass near Highway 14, killing one person and seriously injuring another. Accident occurred in bad weather.

4/15/67. *Piper Cherokee N5840W* hit Cucamonga Peak in bad weather, seriously injuring one person while another escaped with only minor injuries.

Wreck is marked, but may have been removed. No other data available.

7/24/67. *Cessna 210F N1800F* hit power lines in Big Tujunga Canyon at Vogel Flat. Aircraft crashed and burned, killing both persons on board. Wreckage is unmarked and burned. Pilot error is listed as primary cause of crash.

11/28/67. *Cessna 172 N1780F* crashed east of Magic Mountain in Bad Canyon at 4,500' level, killing all three persons on board. Weather was a factor in this accident. Wreck is unmarked.

3/7/68. *Aero Commander N6243B* hit Portal Ridge NW of Lake Hughes in bad weather. No other information available.

3/16/68. *Cessna 150 N6736C* hit ridge two miles west of Mt. Gleason, killing pilot. Only a few parts remain at this site today, which is located on the Pacific Crest Trail. Weather was a factor in this crash.

8/25/68. *Alouette 3* crashed and burned near San Gabriel Dam while on fire-fighting mission. Pilot died in crash.

8/30/68. *Helicopter* crashed two miles north of Cogswell Dam, while on fire-fighting mission, seriously injuring the pilot.

10/2/68. *Cessna 172 N6280E* hit Mt. Harvard in bad weather, killing the pilot. Wreckage is smashed and unmarked.

4/12/69. *Cessna 310 N4011Q* hit Cucamonga Peak at 6,200' level and burned. All five people on board perished in this weather-related accident. Wreck is unmarked.

6/21/69. *Mooney Mk. 21 N3362X* crashed in fog-shrouded Dunsmore Canyon below Mt. Lukens. Three persons died but one person did survive this accident. Wreck is removed.

9/20/69. *Cessna 182 N2640R* hit ridge SW of Palmdale, killing all four on board. Wreck is burned and unmarked.

2/9/70. *Beechcraft Bonanza N618V* hit Iron Mountain at 7,400' level in snowstorm. Although the wreck is intact, it was not survivable for the pilot. Wreck was marked but may have been removed.

3/21/70. *American Yankee* crashed in San Dimas Canyon, killing both men on board. The pilot attempted to fly up a steep canyon in clear weather, but failed to clear the ridge line. Aircraft exploded on impact and burned out completely.

1970. *Piper Cherokee* hit Sunset Peak, killing both persons on board in cloudy weather. Wreck is marked and parts remain visible at 3700' level.

4/20/70. LTV F-8 US Navy crashed in Pine Canyon NW of Palmdale following successful pilot bailout. Wreck is on 4-K Ranch.

5/15/70. *Sikorsky SH-3 US Navy Reserve* crashed on Mt. Disappointment. All three crewmen escaped injury and wreck was removed.

5/17/70. *Monocoupe antique aircraft* force-landed in Vasquez Canyon following engine failure. Pilot escaped unharmed and aircraft was removed.

9/6/70. *Cessna* crashed and burned west of Big Pines, killing two persons on board. Status of wreck today is unknown.

10/70. *Alouette 3* crashed in San Gabriel Canyon, killing all five men on board. Helicopter was on a fire-fighting mission.

4/71. *Piper Comanche* hit a ridge near Acton in bad weather. All four men on board survived and wreck was removed.

5/30/71. *Cessna 210 N948T* hit a ridge near Acton, killing all three persons on board. Weather was a factor in this crash. Wreck is unmarked and parts are visible below Lockheed PV-2 wreck site.

6/6/71. *McDonnell Douglas F-4 USMC* collided with a Hughes Air West DC-9 over Mt. Bliss, killing all fifty persons on the DC-9 and one man on the F-4. The other F-4 crewman ejected but was injured. Scattered wreckage is still visible from both of these aircraft. The DC-9 tail is intact, but very hard to see.

10/4/71. *Sailplane N2265C* hit ridge SW of Mt. Baden-Powell, killing the pilot. Wreck is unmarked and visible.

12/12/71. *Cessna 172* crashed in Newhall Pass, killing all on board. Cloudy weather was a factor in this accident. Wreck is removed.

12/23/71. *Cessna 172* hit mountain south of Newhall in cloudy weather, killing all three people on board. Wreck was removed.

4/5/72. *Cessna 150* crashed in Cougar Canyon near Pacoima Canyon Reservoir without serious injury to the two persons on board. Powerplant failure was listed as cause of accident. Wreck was removed.

5/25/72. *Piper Cherokee R N4546J* crashed in Day Canyon four miles NE of Upland, killing all four on board. Weather was a factor in this crash. Wreck is marked and visible.

10/8/72. *Cessna 172* hit ridge near Acton, killing the four persons on board. Wreck is removed.

3/17/73. *Piper Cherokee* hit ridge near Bouquet Canyon with no fatal injuries to the three persons on board. Accident occurred in cloudy weather. Wreck is removed.

3/21/73. *Cessna 150 N51362* hit mountain in clouds near junction of Highway 14 and Interstate 5. Both persons on board were killed and wreck was removed.

6/2/73. *Cessna 182* hit Libre Mountain near Quail Lake in bad weather. All three persons on board survived without injury.

11/1/73. *Cessna 172* crashed in Wilson Canyon above San Fernando, killing the pilot. Weather was a factor in this crash and wreck was removed.

12/1/73. *Beechcraft 23 N23602* crashed SE Gorman in Libre Mountain area. No other data available.

1/5/74. *Beechcraft Bonanza* hit 2,600' ridge in Little Tujunga Canyon, killing all three persons on board. Wreck is burned and unmarked.

1/74. *Schweizer 2-32* hit ridge west of Baden-Powell seriously injuring both persons on board. Wreck is broken up and unmarked.

5/74. *Bell Jet Ranger of the Los Angeles County Fire Department* crashed in Big Tujunga Canyon, killing one man and seriously injuring two others. Wreck is removed.

6/23/74. *Bell 47* crashed in Big Tujunga Canyon, killing two persons on board. Wreck is removed.

7/25/74. *Lightplane* crashed four miles NW of Wrightwood. Two persons were seriously injured and two others escaped with minor injuries.

10/7/74. *Cessna 205* crashed at 3,200' level of Millard Canyon above Pasadena, killing the pilot. Wreck is removed.

10/28/74. *Globe Swift N4962G* crashed north of San Dimas in mountains, killing the pilot. Status of wreck is not known.

1/21/76. Beechcraft Baron belonging to the Northrop Aircraft Corporation crashed in low hills SE of Pearblossom. Wreckage from this accident that claimed two lives is still visible.

2/15/76. *Piper PA-28 N16330* crashed near Burnt Peak NW of Lake Hughes.

2/29/76. *Piper Cherokee Six N32682* hit Cucamonga Peak at 8,400' level in bad weather, killing all six persons on board. This wreck may have been removed from south slope of mountain.

3/1/76. *Cessna 182 N7916F* fuselage intact at bottom of canyon south of Highway 14 near Bear Canyon.

8/26/76. *Cessna 150 N6200G* crashed just below Highway 2 at Vincent Gap while the pilot was attempting to fly up a canyon. Aircraft struck trees at 6,700' level and broke up. A passing motorist saw wing hanging in tree on 8/27 and stopped to investigate, only to find the badly injured pilot still alive at the base of a tree. The pilot was rescued and this wreck has been removed.

9/15/76. *Cessna 150 N66046* NW of Lake Hughes. No other data available.

10/24/76. *Piper Tri-Pacer N9109* crashed on Vasquez Canyon Road as a result of clear air turbulence. Neither person on board was injured and wreck was removed.

12/23/76. *LTV RF-8G US Navy Reserve* hit Burnt Peak in the Sawmill Mountains, killing the pilot. Wreckage is scattered, burned, and the tail is visible with squadron markings.

4/3/77. *Piper Cherokee* crashed in mountains near Agua Dulce, killing both persons on board. Accident was attributed to a stall/spin. Wreckage removed.

4/16/77. *Beechcraft* crashed in foothills near Quartz Hill. All four persons on board escaped without injury.

Cessna 340
#N98621

Cessna 340 being removed from Noel Canyon near Mendenhall Peak. Crash date is 3/16/83. (NTSB) Region 7.

8/31/77. *Bellanca Viking N4889V* crashed north of San Dimas Golf Course in foothills, killing both people on board. Wreck was removed.

2/12/78. *Cessna 172* hit Cucamonga Peak, killing three, but one person managed to survive in this weather-related accident. Status of wreck unknown.

10/22/78. *Lightplane* with one person on board vanished near Upland and was not located until 4/15/79. Site is in foothills just north of Padua Hills.

11/10/78. *Cessna 172* crashed into north slope of San Sevaine Peak in cloudy weather. All four persons on board survived with minor injuries. Wreckage removed.

1/31/79. *KR-1* flown by its designer Ken Rand crashed on Baldy Mesa at 3,000' level in heavy weather. Rand perished in this crash. Wreck has been removed.

2/19/79. *Cessna 172 N19217V* hit Ontario Peak at 8,200' level on the west slope. Three died but one person survived this weather-related accident.

10/14/79. *Cessna 310* hit Cucamonga Peak in Deer Canyon, killing four and injuring three persons. Some wreckage is still visible at crash site.

1/28/80. *Beechcraft C-45 N7870* crashed in Elsmere Canyon three miles SE of Newhall and one mile north of Antelope Valley Freeway. Two persons perished in this weather-related accident. Wreck has been removed.

2/18/80. *Piper Cherokee* hit ridge near Leona Valley in bad weather. Two persons died, one was seriously hurt, and one escaped with minor injuries. Weather was a factor in this crash. Wreckage is removed.

3/2/80. A *Ryan Navion N2189N* hit Blue Ridge west of Wrightwood in snowstorm. Plane came to rest in Acorn Canyon 100' below crest. All three persons on board escaped without injury. Wreck was removed.

4/27/80. *Piper Turbo-Cherokee* hit mountain near Bear Divide Ranger Station north of San Fernando. One man died in crash. Only a few unmarked parts remain at site today.

8/2/81. *Sailplane N2265C* hit Pinyon Ridge NW of Wrightwood, killing one man. Status of wreck is unknown.

10/28/81. *Cessna 310* hit Los Pinos Peak in cloudy weather, killing all three people on board. Wreckage is removed.

3/13/82. *Cessna 210 N5870F* crashed and burned near Lytle Creek, killing both persons on board. Weather was a factor in this crash.

Date unknown. Schweizer 2-32 N6664 crashed in bottom of the east fork of the San Gabriel River Canyon two miles south of Vincent Gap. Wreckage is visible and unmarked.

3/20/82. *Cessna 340 N98546 SW* of Acton near Bear and Nelson Canyons.

4/10/82. *Cessna 182 N70939* hit Sawtooth Mountain NW of Lake Hughes in bad weather, killing all four people on board. Wreck is visible and marked.

11/30/82. *Cessna 182 N35509K* crashed in east San Gabriel Mountains NW of Fontana.

1/83. *Cessna 140* crashed in heavy snow 500' below Mt. Baldy summit on east slope. The pilot survived with minor injuries and wreckage was removed 6/83.

3/16/83. *Cessna 340 N98621* hit Mendenhall Peak at 4,600' level, killing three persons. Site is located in Noel Canyon and wreck is removed.

3/20/83. *Bell 47* crashed and burned in Big Tujunga Canyon, killing two persons. Weather was a factor in this accident.

10/4/83. *Cessna 185 N8146T* hit Mendenhall Peak, killing the pilot. Accident occurred in cloudy weather. Status of wreck is unknown.

5/25/84. *Sailplane* hit Mt. Lewis, seriously injuring one man. Site is at 6,500' level south of Crystalaire.

10/11/84. *Cessna 210* crashed two miles south of Gorman east of Interstate 5. One person died and one survived with minor injuries. Parts are visible at site.

4/21/85. *Piper Cherokee* crashed two miles east of Interstate 5 in Cherry Canyon, killing all five people on board. Weather was a factor in this crash.

4/21/85. *Cessna 152 N69118* crashed near Gold Creek Road east of Little Tujunga Canyon, killing two persons. Weather was a factor in this accident.

7/19/85. *Piper Archer 2* crashed near Mormon Rocks and junction of Highway 138 in bad weather. Three persons on board perished in crash. Wreck was removed.

3/29/86. A *Beechcraft Bonanza* crashed in the mountains two miles north of Rancho Cucamonga. Both people on board died and some of the wreckage is still visible.

7/28/86. *Sailplane* crashed in foothills south of Pearblossom, killing pilot. Status of wreck today is unknown.

12/3/86. *Bell Jet Ranger* crashed in San Dimas Experimental Forest, slightly injuring pilot. Wreckage was removed.

1/16/87. *Varga Kachina* hit north slope of Mt. San Antonio at 9,200' level, killing both men on board. Downdrafts were a factor in this accident. Wreckage is mostly removed.

2/11/87. *Beechcraft BE-35* crashed in foothills north of Rancho Cucamonga.

Date unknown. *Piper PA-28 N16330* lies wrecked in mountains east of Castaic in Charlie Canyon.

2/14/87. *Cessna 150* crashed in Newhall Pass in bad weather, killing one man. Wreck is removed.

3/87. *Beechcraft Bonanza* hit Monrovia Peak, killing one man. Weather was a factor in this crash. Status of wreck is unknown.

4/2/87. *Champion Citabria* crashed at 4,100' level of Frankish Peak, killing both persons. Wreck is removed.

9/3/87. *Cessna 140* crash landed near Gorman at Quail Lake without injury to pilot. Engine problems were cited as cause and wreck is removed.

10/11/87. *Piper Archer* hit north slope of Mt. San Antonio at 8,900' level, killing all three people on board. Weather was a factor in this crash. Wreck to be removed.

12/87. *Lightplane* hit mountain near Newhall, killing four persons. Weather was a factor in this crash.

10/3/88. *Piper PA-18 N1256A* crashed in mountains ten miles north of Upland, killing two men. Weather was a factor in this accident. Unmarked wreck is burned.

12/31/88. *Piper Pa-28 N5369L* hit top of Mt. San Antonio in snowstorm. Two persons died and one survived this weather-related crash. Wreckage was removed.

5/10/89. *Beechcraft Super King-Air N39YV* hit ridge NE of Crystal Lake in Angeles National Forest. Site is 26 miles north of Azusa. The pilot died in this weather-related crash.

12/27/89. A *Lightplane* crashed near Interstate 5 in bad weather. All four persons on board survived. Site is near Grapevine and wreck is removed.

12/20/90. *Piper PA-28 N6528J* crashed NE of Mt. Wilson near Cogswell.

5/29/90. A *Cessna 182* crashed north of Rancho Cucamonga in cloudy weather. Both persons on board survived with serious injuries. Status of wreck is not known. The Crash site is west of Day Canyon in the rugged chaparral-covered terrain.

9/24/90. *Homebuilt light aircraft* crashed north of Claremont in the foothills of the San Gabriel Mountains, killing both men on board. Wreck is removed and the cause of the accident is under investigation. Weather was apparently not a factor in this crash.

10/13/90. *Piper Cherokee* lost power and crashed after taking off from Agua Dulce airport near Mint Canyon in the Santa Clarita Valley. The two men on board were injured, one of them seriously. Wreck has been removed from hillside impact site.

4/5/92. Two *lightplanes* crashed on Cucamonga Peak in separate accidents in the same mountains. One aircraft is a Champion Citabria N7629S. The pilot of this aircraft survived and was rescued. The pilot of the other unidentified lightplane died. Both crash sites are north of Rancho Cucamonga.

Beechcraft Bonanza N618V crashed on Iron Mountain in bad weather on 2/9/70 killing the pilot. (NTSB) Region 7.

6/30/92. *Erco Ercoupe* crash-landed north of Santa Clarita in San Francisquito Canyon. Both persons on board survived and wreck was removed.

10/11/93. *North American T-6G* from California Civil Air Patrol Condor Squadron crashed near San Francisquito Canyon, killing both men on board. Weather was a factor in this accident. Wreck is removed.

8/13.94. *Lockheed C-130* assigned to USFS for fire-fighting crashed and burned south of Devil's Punch Bowl County Park in the Pallet Mountains region. All three crewmen died in the crash that left wreckage scattered over a wide area.

12/31/95. *Cessna 172 N2569G* crashed in bad weather north of Rancho Cucamonga near Cucamonga Peak. Extensive search effort finally located wreck and the body of the pilot in early 1996. Sadly, three CAP men died while looking for this missing plane. (see below)

1/14/96. *Cessna 182 N9706E* crashed while searching for the *C-172* that had vanished on 12/31/95 near Mt. San Antonio. The three Civil Air Patrol crewmen died when they flew into the 7,700' level of cloud-enshrouded Mt. San Antonio. This book lists more than twenty CAP search aircraft lost while trying to help others in need. As of 7/96, *N9706E* had not been marked or removed.

REGION 8

Region 8 includes the greater Los Angeles Basin and the many hill and mountain systems that lie within it. The Whittier, Covina, and Chino Hills separate the Los Angeles and San Bernardino Basins. Highest point in this area is 1,781' San Juan Hill. To the southwest are the Palos Verdes Hills rising from the Pacific Ocean with a high point of 1,480' on San Pedro Hill. The Santa Monica Mountains are the longest system dividing the San Fernando Valley from Los Angeles proper. These mountains have only a few peaks that rise to 3,000'. East of the Santa Monicas are the Verdugo Mountains with a high point of 3,296' and the San Rafael Hills. To the north and west are the Oat, Oakridge, Santa Susana Mountains, and the Simi and Chatsworth Hills. Highest point in this area is 3,756' Oat Mountain.

The boundaries for this region are: Highways 150, 126, Interstate 210, 66, Interstate 15E in the north, Highways 91, 55, and 73 in the south and east, and the Pacific Ocean in the west.

More than eighty wrecks lie in these often haze and fog obscured hills and mountains of chaparral. Proximity to large population centers has contributed to the removal of most of Region 8s crash sites.

11/26/27. *Ryan mail plane* crashed near Castaic following pilot bail-out in bad weather. Status of wreck is unknown

Date unknown. *Biplane* crashed in San Rafael hills near Rose Bowl site. Wreck was removed.

3/5/30. *Travelaire 4000* crashed in the Santa Monica Mountains between Bone and Milt Canyons. Three men died in the crash. The plane did not burn and parts were visible at the site for many years. Weather was a factor in this accident.

5/5/31. *Boeing Model 40* hit Verdugo Mountains in foggy conditions, killing both men on board. Wreck was removed. This aircraft belonged to Pacific Air Transport and was used as a mail plane.

12/28/36. *Boeing 247D NC-13355 of United Air Transport* crashed in Rice Canyon west of Newhall in Oat Mountains. Weather was a factor in this

Douglas R4D US Navy crashed and burned in the Santa Monica Mtns. killing all seven on board. Crash date was 7/13/49. Fog was a factor. (D. Hatfield) Region 8.

crash that killed twelve people. Wreck is marked in bottom of canyon and was visible until it was removed in 1994.

Date unknown. *Old 1930s wreckage* reported at China Flat south of Simi Valley. Possible Ford Tri-motor.

11/12/43. A *Vultee BT-13 USAAF* hit the north slope of the Palos Verdes Hills near Chadwick School, killing both men on board. Crash occurred in foggy conditions. Wreck was completely removed.

6/2/44. *Lockheed P-38L USAAF* crashed on Palos Verdes Peninsula following pilot bail-out. Site is above Point Fermin and is 98 percent removed.

7/15/44. Lockheed P-38 USAAC crashed in McCoy Canyon west of Woodland Hills in the Santa Monica Mountains. Pilot was killed in this clear-weather, pilot-error accident. Wreck was covered over.

1/11/45. *Douglas DC-3 NC-25684* of American Airlines crashed in Verdugo Mountains, killing all twenty-four persons on board. Few parts remain at the unmarked crash site in McClure Canyon. Weather was a factor in this accident.

1945. *Beechcraft C-45* hit ridge above Brand Park in Verdugo Mountains, killing five or six persons. Weather was a factor in the crash. Only the engines and a few small parts remain in the canyon below the impact site.

3/17/46. *Luscombe 8 NC-45511* crashed in Santa Ynez Canyon north of Santa Monica injuring two persons. This weather-related wreck was removed.

1946. *Stinson 105 NR45089* hit ridge and burned just below Mulholland Drive in Santa Monica Mountains. Site is 1/2 mile west of Topanga Canyon. Wreckage was visible for many years, but is now removed.

4/15/47. *Vultee BT-13 NC-67244* crashed on south slope of Mt. Hollywood in cloudy weather, killing both people on board. Wreck was removed from this Santa Monica Mountain crash site.

7/1/47. *Biplane, single seat NR-45089* crashed near the top of Beverly Glen at Mulholland Drive. Pilot escaped with minor injuries, wreck was removed.

8/28/47. A *Douglas A-26 NC-37493* hit the east slope of Verdugo Mountains in Deer Canyon, killing all three on board. Accident occurred in cloudy weather. Wreck is burned and mostly removed.

12/12/47. *Stearman PT-13 NC-57215* crashed on Oat Mountain without injury to pilot. Intact wreck was reported visible for many years. Status today is probably removed.

7/13/49. *Curtiss C-46 N79978* of New Standard Airlines hit Chatsworth Peak, killing many crew and passengers. Survivors, however, claimed that the flight crew were engaged in a fist-fight at the time of the crash. Only a few parts remain at crash site today.

7/13/49. *Douglas R4D US Navy* hit Santa Monica Mountains in cloudy weather three miles north of Sunset Blvd. Crash site is in Dry Canyon, burned and unmarked. Seven Navy men died in this accident.

9/11/50. *Lockheed C-60 Loadstar* crashed in mountains two mile west of the Chatsworth, killing all on board. Wreck is silver, scattered, and marked with a yellow X on rock face.

12/20/50. *North American F-51D California Air Guard* hit north slope of Santa Monica Mountains, killing pilot. Site was in lower Coldwater Canyon, and is removed.

2/12/51. *Grumman Widgeon* hit Saddle Peak in the Santa Monica Mountains, killing two men on board in cloudy weather. Wreck was removed from 1,100' level crash site.

3/6/52. *Howard DGA NC-68700* Air-ambulance crashed in Chino Hills near Diamond Bar, killing all five persons on board. Accident occurred in cloudy weather and the crash site is located in Rodeo Canyon in heavy brush and trees. Although unmarked, this wreck was undisturbed for many years near Tonner Canyon in Orange County.

4/18/52. *C-46 NC-3404C North Continent Airlines* crashed in Whittier Hills near Rose Hills, killing all twenty-nine people on board. Accident occurred in cloudy weather. Wreck was removed.

12/52. *Lockheed Loadstar N50651* crashed into east slope of Verdugo Mountains near Sun Valley, killing all five people on board. Weather was a factor in this accident. Only a few unmarked parts remain at this site today.

12/21/52. *Aeronca L3C N48816* crashed in bad weather west of Newhall in Weldon Canyon. One person died in crash. Site is in Oat Mountains and is unmarked.

Date unknown. *Northrop F-89C USAF* crashed and burned in Chino Hills following wing separation. One man died in crash. Wreck was removed. Aircraft was on test flight from Northrop facility at Ontario Airport.

6/29/53. *North American AT-6 #209 of the California Air Guard* crashed in the Santa Monica Mountains 1/2 mile east of Pluma Road on Saddle Peak. Both crewmen were seriously injured and aircraft was removed.

4/20/54. *Fairchild C-119 USAF* hit Mission Point in the Santa Susana Mountains, killing all seven on board. Wreckage is burned, mostly removed, and unmarked.

5/16/54. Lockheed T-33B US Navy hit Sulfur Mountain SE of Ojai, killing both crewmen. Wreck is unmarked and visible on south slope.

Date unknown. *North American F-86F USAF* crashed east of Camarillo near Conejo Mountain. Wreck was removed.

Date unknown. *Aircraft type unknown* crashed on Conejo Ridge near Thousand Oaks.

Date unknown. *Cessna 140* crashed in Santa Monica Mountains near Malibu, killing the two persons on board. Wreck is removed from site.

Date unknown. *Cessna 195* hit peak at west end of Santa Monica Mountains. Wreck is unmarked and mostly removed.

1/31/57. *Northrop F-89D USAF* collided with Douglas DC-7C over Pacoima and crashed in Verdugo Mountains. One man died and one bailed out. Site is in La Tuna Canyon and is scattered and unmarked. The DC-7C crashed, causing heavy loss of life in a Pacoima school yard.

4/15/57. *Piper Pacer N5604H* crashed in hills near Ventura, killing the pilot. Weather was a factor in this accident. Wreck has been removed.

4/16/57. *Fairchild PT-23* crashed and burned in Santa Monica Mountains north of Leo Carillo State Beach. Both persons on board perished in this weather-related accident. Wreck is not visible today.

8/15/59. *Beechcraft Bonanza N3846N* crashed in Santa Monica Mountains below Mulholland Drive and above the Encino Reservoir. Four persons died in this weather-related crash. Wreckage is still visible today.

Douglas A-26 NC-37493 crashed in bad weather and burned in the Verdugo Mountains near Burbank on 8/28/47. (D. Hatfield) Region 8.

8/15/59. A *Aeronca Champion 7FC N9055B* crash landed on Palos Verdes following engine failure. Two persons on board sustained only minor injuries and wreck was removed.

12/15/59. *Beechcraft Bonanza N3739N* hit Palos Verdes Hills near High Ridge Road, killing two men. Weather was a factor in the accident, and wreck is removed.

10/25/60. *Beechcraft Bonanza N80439* crashed and burned in hills west of Santa Paula, killing one man. Aircraft went down in cloudy weather. Part of wreckage is still visible in O'Hare Canyon.

6/27/61. *Beechcraft Model 50* crashed in Chino Hills on Double S Ranch. All three men on board died in this weather-related accident. Status of wreck is unknown.

8/25/61. *Douglas AD-5 #33876 US Navy* crashed in the Puente Hills and burned. Wreck is unmarked and mostly removed.

9/21/61 *Douglas C-47 USAF* hit north slope of Oat Mountain in cloudy weather, killing three and seriously injuring three crewmen. This wreck is mostly removed.

5/3/63. *Martin B-57E #55-4296 USAF* crashed in low coastal hills near Rincon NW of Ventura. Both crewmen died in the crash and wreckage is scattered and visible.

1963. *DeHavilland Mosquito N9919F* crashed in Las Virgenes Canyon, killing the pilot who bailed out too low in what was thought to be a "bomb on board" murder plot, but may have been hydraulic fire. Aircraft was burned and removed from Simi Hills site.

1/17/64. *Cessna 310 N5281A* crashed in Simi Hills near Agoura, killing two persons on board. Scattered wreckage is visible at site today. Accident was weather-related.

9/19/64. *Cessna 172 N8025X* crashed in Santa Monica Mountains 1/2 mile north of Mount Saint Mary's College. Four people died in this weather-related accident. Wreckage has been completely removed.

1964. *Cessna 172* hit north slope of Mt. Hollywood in Santa Monica Mountains. Two persons died in this weather-related crash. Wreck is removed.

12/26/64. *Piper Pacer N5859H* crashed in Whittier Hills, killing two people. The wreck of this weather-related accident has been removed.

Date unknown. *McDonnell F-4 US Navy* hit Mesa Peak in Santa Monica Mountains, killing both crewmen. Wreckage is scattered and unmarked.

2/26/65. *Aerocoupe N3720H* crashed in Oakridge Mountains during a rain storm. One person died and one survived in this accident. Status of wreck today is not known.

10/2/66. *Beechcraft Model 50* crashed and burned in Santa Monica Mountains west of lower Topanga Canyon. Wreck is located 1/2 mile from beach and parts are still visible. Two persons died in this weather-related accident.

4/15/67. *Cessna 150 N4181U* crashed in Oat Mountains in bad weather, killing one person and injuring another. Site is four miles SW of Newhall and is removed.

10/1/68. *Hughes 269 of Los Angeles Sheriff's Department* crashed in Whittier Hills, killing both crewmen. Wreck was removed.

4/16/69. *Cessna 177 N30452* crashed in Chino Hills, killing both persons on board. Wreck is removed. Weather was listed as a cause of the accident.

6/29/69. *Piper Clipper* crashed near Diamond Bar in Chino Hills, killing both persons on board. Wreckage is burned and removed. Pilot error was listed as cause of this accident.

1/10/70. *Cessna 150 N22390* crashed in Temescal Canyon of the Santa Monica Mountains, killing both persons on board. Site is 1.5 miles north of Sunset Blvd. Wreck has been removed in this weather-related accident.

1/13/70. *Beechcraft Bonanza N2124D* hit south slope of Oat Mountain in bad weather, killing the pilot. Some parts remain at site today.

3/6/70. *Cessna 172 N770LW* crashed in Carbon Canyon of the Santa Monica Mountains. All four persons on board survived without serious injury. Pilot error was listed as cause of crash and wreck was removed.

Date unknown. *Cessna 152 N49216* crashed and burned in the Oak Ridge Mountains south of Santa Paula.

3/30/70. *Beechcraft Bonanza* crashed in Chino Hills near Carbon Canyon Dam. Pilot died in this weather-related accident.

5/19/73. *Aero Commander 560* crashed in Bee Canyon near Porter Ranch. Pilot died in this weather-related accident. Wreckage was completely burned.

3/10/74. *Cessna 150* hit ridge near Moorpark Community College, killing one and seriously injuring another person on board. Wreck is removed.

3/17/74. *Cessna 172* hit power lines near Santa Paula in bad weather, killing all four persons on board. Crash site in hills was completely consumed by fire.

4/21/74. *Piper Cub* hit mountain peak south of Santa Paula, killing the pilot. Weather was a factor in this crash.

2/5/76. *Cessna* crashed in Santa Susana Mountains above Van Norman Dam, seriously injuring the pilot. Weather was a factor in this crash.

2/26/78. *Piper Cherokee* crashed in Santa Susana Mountains, killing all four

Curtiss C-46 N79928 belonging to New Stanford Airlines crashed on Chatsworth Peak in the Simi Hills. Date of accident was 7/13/49. (D. Hatfield) Region 8.

on board. Crash site is on L.A./Ventura County Line. Weather was a factor in this accident.

3/2/78. *Fairchild-Republic-Hiller F-105G USAF* crashed in hills near Newbury Park, killing one and injuring one crewmen. Wreck was removed and accident was attributed to malfunction.

4/15/78. *Cessna 172* hit 3,300' level of Oat Mountain, killing both persons on board.

4/80. A *Temco Swift* crashed in a canyon west of Moorpark College near the town of Moorpark. The pilot had purchased the plane the week before, was doing low-level aerobatics with a passenger and misjudged his height above the ground. The plane struck the ground out of the bottom of a loop and disintegrated. The passenger was thrown clear and survived! The pilot was not so fortunate. The wreck was removed by the FAA the following day.

3/13/85. *Mooney Mk. 20* hit power lines at Mission Point in Santa Susana Mountains, killing both persons on board. Wreckage is burned. Weather was a factor in this crash.

5/27/86. *Piper Cherokee Dakota* hit 800' ridge in Chino Hills, killing all four persons on board. Crash was weather-related and wreck was removed.

7/21/86. *Piper Cub* crashed in south Chino Hills, killing one person and seriously injuring another. Pilot error was listed as cause of crash.

6/18/87. *Cessna 172* crashed in Latigo Canyon near Malibu in Santa Monica Mountains. Both people on board escaped injury in this pilot-error accident. Wreck is removed.

12/19/87. *Beechcraft Twin and Cessna lightplane* collided over the Chino Hills, killing both pilots. Crash sites are located two miles west of State Highway 71 in southern Chino Hills. Wrecks are removed.

8/2/88. *Cessna 210* crashed while flying in low clouds in Chino Hills. Pilot died in crash. Site is located in Carbon Canyon area of Chino Hills State Park. Wreck is burned and removed.

Date unknown. *Cessna 152 N24257* crashed SW of Newhall in the Santa Susana Mountains.

2/22/90. *Siai Marchetti SF-260* crashed near Malibu Creek State Park in the

Santa Monica Mountains, killing both men on board. Aircraft may have been engaged in aerobatic flying at time of crash. Wreck is removed.

3/10/90. *Piper Cherokee* hit hillside near Malibu in foggy weather, killing all four persons on board. Wreck is removed.

6/90. *Cessna 172* crashed in rugged area of Topanga Canyon of the Santa Monica Mountains. The Cessna struck a ridge in cloudy weather and exploded, killing all four people on board. Wreck is burned and unmarked.

1991. *Piper Cherokee* hit ridge near Brand Park in Verdugo Mountains, killing a student pilot. Wreckage was removed from Mt. Tom crash site.

11/16/93. *Piper Twin Commanche* crashed near Carbon Canyon Road in the Chino Hills. The pilot died in this crash and the wreckage was removed.

3/28/96. *"Fly Boy" homebuilt aircraft* crashed in mountains just east of Interstate 5 at Templen Highway. Pilot survived and wreck was removed.

5/28/58 Following pilot bail-out, a North American F-86L crashed west of Avalon on Santa Catalina Island. Unmarked wreck still visible. (G.P. Macha) Region 9.

Region 9

Region 9 includes the Channel Islands located off the Southern California coast. Five of these islands are part of the Channel Islands National Monument. They are: Anacapa, Santa Barbara, Santa Cruz, San Miguel, and Santa Rosa. San Clemente and San Nicholas Islands are US military reservations and are closed to public access. Santa Catalina is the most accessible of all the Channel Islands with a conservancy responsible for all of the area, except the square mile city of Avalon. Approximately thirty crash sites dot these islands.

Anacapa

Date unknown. *Grumman F4F* is reported to have crashed on West Anacapa Island. No wreckage visible today. Aircraft was supposed to be USMC lost during WW II.

1/6/89. *Cessna 150* crashed on West Anacapa Island, killing both persons on board. Wreck was located 1/24/89 and removed shortly thereafter.

Santa Catalina Island

1921. *Curtiss Flying Boat US Navy* hit headland south of Avalon, killing all three men on board. Wreck was removed.

5/6/42. *Lockheed P-38D #40-774 USAAC* crashed on training flight at Buffalo Springs near airport. This aircraft was flown by Second Lieutenant Walter F. Lichtenberger of the 94th Pursuit Squadron, based at March Field in Riverside County. Lt. Lichtenberger was killed when he misjudged his recovery from a shallow dive. The wreck was accidentally burned during salvage operations and no visible wreckage remains at site today.

10/17/44. *Goodyear Blimp US Navy* hit 1,600' ridge west of Avalon while on anti-submarine patrol in low clouds and fog. Six crewmen died and five survived with serious injuries. Gondola and engines remain at crash site, partly overgrown by chaparral.

1944-45. *Vought F4U US Navy* collided with *PBY* and crashed on east end of island. Pilot bailed out but drowned in kelp. Wreck did not burn and

Teledyne Ryan Firebee Drone

While surveying a Vought F4U-4 site on Santa Cruz Island we found a Teledyne Ryan Firebee Drone at the bottom of a steep canyon. Gary Salazar inspects the turbo-jet engine. (G.P. Macha) Region 9.

came to rest upside down and intact. In 1970s, Marine helicopters picked up most of wreck and dumped it in the ocean. A few parts remain at site today.

1946-47. *Grumman TBM US Navy Reserve* reported to have crashed near Mt. Orizaba NW of Avalon while on training flight from Los Alamitos Naval Air Station. Scattered unmarked parts were still visible as of 2/96.

Late 1940s. Two *Grumman TBF Avengers US Navy Reserve* crashed near west end of island in cloudy weather. Both pilots died and both wrecks remained easily visible until partial salvage by USMC helicopters in 1970s. Engine, landing gear, and other parts are still at site near Parson's Landing.

5/28/58. *North American F-86L USAF* crashed west of Avalon following in-flight malfunction. North American Aviation test pilot Bill Yoakley bailed out successfully and landed in the ocean. Unmarked wreckage still visible in canyon three miles west of Avalon. The pilot was rescued from the water.

5/31/67. A *Cessna 150 N8634S* crashed in box canyon at 1,000' level near airport. Both persons survived with injuries in this pilot-error accident. Wreck is removed.

1/10/69. *McDonnell Douglas F-4B US Navy* hit top of ridge west of Avalon, killing both crewmen. Ridge top is impregnated with wreckage, and scattered debris covers more than one acre. Pilot had been buzzing Avalon at time of crash.

2/18/69. A *Grumman E-1B US Navy* hit Silver Peak near west end of island in bad weather, killing the five-man crew. Wreckage is visible in canyon leading down to Ironbound Bay.

3/21/72. *Cessna 150* crashed at base of Palisades near Silver Canyon, killing both men on board. Wreck is not removed nor is it marked.

8/22/77. *Beechcraft Model 18* hit mountain near Long Point at 1,000' level in cloudy weather. Two men on board died in crash. Wreck is removed.

2/21/82. *Cessna 172* crashed near Cactus Peak on the SW side of Catalina Island. All four persons on board survived with minor injuries. Status of wreck is not known.

5/20/84. *Piper Lance* crashed two miles north of airport, killing two persons and injuring three. Wreck is removed.

1/18/85. *McDonnell Douglas F-18 US Navy* hit mountain at 600' level near White's Point, killing the pilot. Accident occurred at night with stratus clouds present. Wreck is removed.

2/16/93. *Lightplane* crashed in mountains near center of the island, killing two persons. Wreck is mostly removed.

4/6/94. *Cessna 152* crashed two miles west of "The Airport In The Sky", killing the pilot. Wreck is removed.

Note. *Many accidents* have occurred adjacent to airport and are not listed here. Also a number of seaplanes wrecks are located under water near Avalon, including a *Sikorsky S-43* at Hamilton Cove. Other underwater wrecks include: Republic Seabee at White Cove, Grumman F6F and Fleetwings Seabird off Avalon.

San Clemente Island

Date unknown. *US Navy wreck* or wrecks at north end of island, dating from 1930s. Type or types of aircraft unknown.

1960. *Douglas C-54 or C-117D USN* crashed near Mt. Thirst in dense fog, killing many persons. Wreck still visible.

1978-79. A *Lightplane* crashed on the island, killing the pilot. Plane was missing for more than one year.

Santa Cruz Island

1924-28. Wreckage of *"Prohibition Era" bootleg aircraft* crashed on beach NW of Christy's Ranch. Wreckage is covered by run-off mud and silt from nearby cliffs. Wheel hubs and few parts remain visible at the surface. Excavation of this historic site should prove to be very interesting. Site is 200 yards north of *Cessna 182B N7254E.*

3/4/49. *Vought F4U-4 USMC #97448* crashed on Santa Cruz in bad weather, killing the pilot. Wreck is scattered and unmarked west of Scorpion Ranch on Barren Ridge.

9/30/63. A *Cessna 150 N71159* crashed on SW side of island. No other information available.

3/8/66. *Piper Cherokee Six N3296W* crashed in bad weather on Santa Cruz Island, killing all six persons on board. Status of crash site is mostly removed.

3/8/66. *Cessna 182B N7254E* crashed on Santa Cruz Island, killing the pilot. Wreckage is visible and scattered at NW side of island, 200 yards south of old bootleg plane near Christy's Ranch.

1970s. *Lockheed QT-33A USN* based at NAS Pt. Mugu crashed on Picacho Diablo, killing the pilot. Wreckage is unmarked and partly removed.

1974. A *Cessna 150 N71159* crash landed on Poso Beach. Both pilot and passenger survived after low-flying plane was hit by a large wave and hit beach where 90 percent of the wreckage is buried by sand!

Date unknown. *Ryan Firebee Drone* lies unmarked and intact 1/4 mile west of USMC F4U-4 in deep canyon.

1/18/84. *Cessna 206* crashed on east end of island, seriously injuring three persons on board. Status of wreck today not known.

Date unknown. *Cessna 337* is wrecked near Pelican Bay. No other data available.

1985. *Lightplane* crashed on SE side of island without injury to the pilot. Wreck is removed.

9/91. During an aircraft wreckage survey of Santa Cruz Island, an unexploded *Raytheon AIM-7 Sparrow missile* was discovered six miles SE of Christy's Ranch near Canada Rosa. In 10/91 a US Navy demolition crew removed the missile and its warhead.

San Miguel Island

7/5/43. *Consolidated B-24E #42-7180 USAAF* crashed on Green Mountain. Wreck is scattered, partly burned, and unmarked. Twelve men died in this weather- related accident. This aircraft was not located until 3/19/44, even though military personnel were based on the island less than a mile from the crash site. This site requires special permission from the National Park

5/6/42. Lockheed P-381D #40-774 USAAF crashed near Buffalo Springs, Catalina Island. The pilot died in this wartime training accident. (G.P. Macha) Region 9.

Service to visit. Nothing can be removed from this WW II monument, according to Park Service regulations.

Santa Rosa Island

1950s. *Stinson 105 Voyager N67100* lies wrecked on island dry lake bed upside down. One man died and three were injured in this accident.

1950s. *Piper Pacer NC5582H* is wrecked and is unmarked near Johnson's Lee.

1950s. *North American F-51D USAF* crashed NE Carrington Point. No other data available.

1970s. *Stinson L-5* crashed next to Agustin Canyon. Wreckage is still visible.

Santa Barbara Island

Two *lightplanes* have force landed on Santa Barbara Island and both have been removed. The broken wooden propeller once reported on the island has long since been removed.

San Nicholas Island

1940s. Two *US Navy aircraft* crashed near the airfield and scattered unmarked parts remain visible today. One wreck is a Consolidated PB4Y-2 that hit a shear cliff and exploded.

1950s. Four *Grumman F6F-5Ks US Navy target drones* crashed on various parts of the island. One of these aircrafts is intact at the NW corner of San Nicholas Island and is #79063 from Point Mugu Naval Weapons Station. The tail of this aircraft is marked with the number five.

1970s. *North American QF-86H US Navy drone aircraft* lies broken up and unmarked near end of runway.

1980s. *LTV A-7 US Navy aircraft* crashed on San Nicholas Island. No other data available.

Region 10

Region 10 includes all of Santa Barbara County and most of Ventura County. The mountain systems included within this area are not of great height, but they are rugged and steep.

Region 10 is bounded on the west by the Pacific Ocean, on the south by Highways 150 and 126, on the east by Interstate 5, on the north by Highway 168. The highest peak in Ventura County is 8,831' Mt. Pinos. The highest point in Santa Barbara County is 6,828' Big Pine Mountain. Some of the mountain ranges located in Region 10 are: Sierra Madre, San Rafael, Santa Ynez, and the imposing Topatopa Mountains. Within this region are more than 90 wreck sites.

1920s. *Curtiss J4N "Jenny"* is located on the SE slope of Refugio Pass above El Capitan State Beach. Wreck is overgrown by chaparral.

2/1/32. *Stinson SM6000B Tri-motor NC-10813 of Century Pacific Airlines* crashed four miles NW of Lebec in bad weather, killing all eight persons on board. Wreckage is mostly removed. Site is in San Emigdio Mountains.

9/19/42. *US Marine aircraft* crashed in cloudy weather on west slope of coastal mountains near Goleta. No other information is available.

9/20/42. *US Marine aircraft* crashed while circling mountain crash site of previous day near Goleta. Both crewmen were killed. Status of wreck today is unknown.

Date unknown. *Vought F4U USMC* crashed SW of Buellton in Santa Ynez Mountains. Wreck is unmarked but mostly intact. Efforts to remove this wreck began in 1989.

Date unknown. *Grumman F4F USMC* west of Refugio Pass is hard to see, unmarked, and burned. Site is in Santa Ynez Mountains, and is reported removed.

Date unknown. *Consolidated B-24E #43-7011 USAAF* crashed near Little Pine Mountain near Gibraltar Dam in Camusa Canyon in bad weather, killing two crewmen who bailed out over the ocean and drowned. Eight

Engine from T-6G N188C

The author and Pratt & Whitney R-1340-47 engine from T-6G N188C. (P. J. Macha) Region 10.

other crewmen bailed out successfully over land. Wreck is scattered and unmarked.

Date unknown. *Grumman F4F US Navy* hit the south slope of Mt. Pinos, killing pilot. Accident occurred in bad weather. Wreck is unmarked and burned.

Date unknown. *North American P-51D USAAF* hit mountain near Nordhoff Peak east of Wheeler Springs, killing pilot. Site is unmarked and partly removed.

2/27/43. *Douglas C-47 USAAF* towing *Waco CG-4A #42-78927* lost tail in severe turbulence and crashed NW of Castaic in the low hills. One wing is visible today at the site and it is unmarked. Waco made a safe landing but all perished aboard the C-47. The cause of the crash is still unknown.

Date unknown. Two *Lockheed P-38L USAAF fighters* collided over Matilija Canyon. No other data available.

3/31/44. *Lockheed P-38 USAAF* crashed and burned seven miles NE of Fillmore near Oak Flat Forest station. The pilot died in this accident and wreckage is removed.

Date unknown. Two *Lockheed P-38 USAAF fighters* crashed on Los Coches Mountain east of Santa Maria. One wreck site is located low on the mountain on Suey Ranch, the other wreck is near the 3,016' summit, is marked, and visible.

Date unknown. *Vultee BT-13 USAAC* hit ridge and burned east of Topatopa Peak. Wreck is unmarked and difficult to see.

6/18/45. *US Marine aircraft* hit mountain near Santa Barbara in cloudy weather, killing the pilot who was commander of MCVG-7. No other data available.

Date unknown. *Vought F4U* crashed in rolling hills west of Buellton. Property owner buried this mostly intact wreck. Parts are still visible at site.

Date unknown. *North American SNJ-6 #112353 US Navy* crashed NW of Peak Mountain in the Sierra Madre Mountains. The wreck is marked and visible.

11/14/46. *Douglas DC-3 NC-18645 Western Airlines* hit White Mountain in bad weather, killing all on board. Wreck is visible at 6,000' level on east slope of mountain and is visible from Interstate 5. The site is unmarked and difficult to reach on foot.

11/17/46. *Aeronca* crashed on search flight for *DC-3 NC-18645* hitting Topatopa Peak, seriously injuring pilot. Wreck is unmarked and difficult to see.

12/22/47. Two *Grumman F6F US Navy* collided near Highway 99 at Holland Summit. Both pilots died in crash. Scattered unmarked parts remain at impact sites.

Date unknown. *Douglas C-47* crashed west of Mt. Pinos in Grouse Mountain area. No other data available.

Date unknown. *North American T-6* crashed and burned SE of Topatopa Peak. Site is unmarked. May be Vultee BT-13.

1949. *Culver V NC44696* crashed in bad weather on east slope of Topatopa Peak. Wreck is marked and intact as pilot escaped with only minor injuries.

Date unknown. *Lightplane* hit Hildreth Peak and is unmarked.

Date unknown. *Stinson 108* crashed east of Highway 33 and south of Ventucopa. Wreck is unmarked.

4/6/51. *Douglas DC-3 NC-63107 Pacific Southwest Airlines* hit north slope of Santa Ynez Peak, killing all twenty-two people on board. Weather was a factor in this accident. Wreckage has been bulldozed over.

Date unknown. *Piper Crusier NC-3502M* crashed on Santa Ynez Peak. Wreck is unmarked and overgrown on north side of slope.

Date unknown. *Aeronca Defender* on Devil's Heart Peak in Topatopa Mountains. Visible on north slope.

Date unknown. *Lockheed P-38L USAAF* crash-landed on the dry bed of the Santa Maria River north of Sisquoc. Wreck is mostly buried by sediment and is unmarked.

Date unknown. *Vultee BT-13* civil registration is visible, partly intact east of Hines Peak above west fork of Sespe River.

Date unknown. *Beechcraft Bonanza* with old civil registration on ridge east of Bear Heaven. Wreck is unmarked.

Date Unknown. *Cessna 140 NC-72335* crashed on north slope of Santa Ynez Peak. Site is marked but overgrown.

Date unknown. *Piper Cub* crashed north of Rincon on Monte Arido. Site is unmarked and possibly removed.

Date unknown. *Cessna 120 (?) NC-77497* crashed and burned north of Lake Cachuma. No other data available.

1953. *Aeronca* crashed after hitting a ridge north of Frazier Park. No other data available.

Date unknown. *Douglas AD-5 US Navy NE* of Ojai in Hobo Canyon. Unmarked parts only.

Date unknown. Ryan Navion crashed in mountains east of Ventucopa. No other data available.

Date unknown. *Cessna 170* crashed near Hines Peak north of Santa Paula, killing all on board. Wreck is visible and marked.

1957. *Vultee BT-13 N63118* Civil Air Patrol crashed on Thorn Peak in the rugged Topatopa Mountains. Both crewmen died in the crash while engaged in a search mission. Wreck is marked.

1957. *Lockheed T-33 US Navy* hit Blue Ridge near Brush Mountain west of Frazier Park. The pilot died in this weather-related accident. One wing remains visible at this unmarked site.

9/20/59. *Cessna UC-78 N54681* crashed on Mt. Pinos without serious injury to any of the five people on board. This aircraft was removed.

12/20/59. *Cessna 182 N21226* hit the north slope of Frazier Peak, killing all

Propellor hub and engine parts of NAA P-51D aircraft that crashed on Nordhoff Peak. (P.J. Macha) Region 10.

Cessna 150
N4588U

Cessna 150 crashed while flying up a steep canyon in the Topatopa Mtns. north of Santa Paula. Incredibly, both pilot and passenger survived with minor injuries. (Glen H. Sexton) Region 10.

four persons on board. Weather was a factor in this crash. Status of wreck today is unknown.

12/20/59. *McDonnell F4H-1* crashed on test flight from Edwards AFB six miles SW of Frazier Park killing the pilot. Wreck status is unknown.

10/9/60. *Beechcraft Model 50 N5683D* crashed in bad weather east of Highway 33 near Ozena Guard Station. Wreck is unmarked and burned over. At least one person died in this accident.

4/18/61. *Lockheed T-33A USAF* crashed in Oak Flats Canyon about five miles north of Fillmore. Two crewmen died in this weather-related crash. Wreck is scattered and unmarked.

8/24/61. *North American T-6G USFS* hit SW slope of Frazier Mountain, killing both men on board. Parts remain visible at 7,000' level and are unmarked. A rattlesnake in the cockpit is the factor that may have caused this plane to crash. Some salvage is reported on this wreck in 1994.

Date unknown. *Ryan Navion* is reported wrecked and unmarked in the Sand Hills west of Santa Maria.

6/19/62. *Cessna N3142B* crashed in cloudy weather NE of Santa Ynez in low hills, killing all four on board. Wreck has been removed.

9/4/63. *Ercoupe N7506C* hit La Cumbre Peak near Santa Barbara in cloudy weather, killing the pilot. This wreck is visible and unmarked. Crash site is at 3,000' level.

11/19/63. *Cessna 170 N2507V* crashed near Little Pine Mountain, killing the pilot. Accident occurred in bad weather and status of wreck today is unknown.

7/8/64. *Sikorsky UH-34D #145714 US Navy* lies wrecked on north slope of Topatopa Peak. Wreck is unmarked and has a white number 5 on its side.

8/24/64. *Cessna 150 N1392F* is burned and unmarked near the west fork of the Sespe River. Two persons died in this pilot-error accident.

12/31/64. *Cessna 182 N9256X* is wrecked near Pine Mountain Ridge east of Highway 33.

12/31/64. *Piper Twin Commanche N7023W* crashed 1.5 miles west of Lebec, killing all five people on board. Weather was a factor in this crash. All wreckage has been removed.

2/28/65. *Cessna 150 N4588U* crashed north of Santa Paula in Topatopa Mountains. Wreck is marked, intact and visible. Both persons on board escaped serious injury in this pilot-error accident.

3/15/65. *Beechcraft Bonanza N840R* crashed six miles north of Frazier Park in canyon, killing one and seriously injuring two persons. Only a few parts remain at this unmarked weather-related site.

3/16/65. *Lightplane* crashed four miles south of Frazier Park, killing both persons on board. Weather was a factor in this crash. All wreckage has been removed.

4/13/65. *Beechcraft Model 50* crashed four miles east of San Marcos Pass north of Santa Barbara. One man died in this weather-related accident. Wreck is partly removed and unmarked.

8/5/65. *Lockheed P-38 N504M* crashed and burned in Foxen Canyon nine miles north of Buelton. Pilot died in unsuccessful bailout attempt following systems malfunction. Wreck is unmarked in gully on private land and was reported removed as of 1/91.

11/26/65. *Cessna 150 N1270Y* is located on Whiteacre Peak north of Piru. Wreck is visible and marked.

5/28/66. Lightplane crashed in hills north of Solvang and east of Highway 101. No other data available.

Date unknown. *Cessna 172 N19659* crashed east of Highway 33 near Ballinger Canyon Campground.

6/13/66. *Cessna 180 N3151C* crashed and burned in Wellman Canyon, killing two men and injuring two others. This accident touched off a major fire in Los Padres National Forest. Pilot error was listed as cause of crash.

4/28/67. A *Cessna 150 N6282T* crashed in canyon SW of Frazier Park in bad weather. Pilot survived with minor injuries. Wreckage is unmarked and difficult to see.

9/24/67. A *Piper Tri-Pacer N1439C* crashed in Santa Ynez Mountains north of Carpinteria, killing both persons on board. Weather was a factor in this accident.

9/27/68. *Piper Cherokee* hit Santa Ynez Peak SE of Solvang, killing two people on board. Wreck was located 10/2/68 and is now marked but hard to see. Weather was a factor in this crash.

11/11/68. *Lightplane* crashed in Los Padres National Forest. Two persons survived with minor injuries. No other data available.

1/15/69. *Cessna 150 N8437J* crashed in Santa Ynez Mountains NE of Carpinteria. The pilot escaped with minor injuries in this weather-related accident.

6/1/70. *Cessna 150* is wrecked in Santa Ynez Mountains west of Highway 101 in Gaviota Pass.

5/29/71. *Cessna 182 N2147G* flown by retired USAF General William O. Hunziker and his wife hit Hines Peak at 6,500' level in cloudy weather. Both perished in this weather-related accident. Wreck is intact, unburned, and clearly visible from air. Date located was 6/6/71.

11/14/71. *Piper PA-28 N3626R* is wrecked on north slope of Santa Ynez Mountains Site is SE of Santa Ynez Airport.

8/26/72. *Bell Model 206* crashed on ridge near Hines Peak in Topatopa Mountains. Six men died and five survived during fire-fighting mission. Status of wreck is unknown.

11/11/72. *Beechcraft Bonanza N7953M* crashed in bad weather eight miles from Santa Ynez Airport in Aliso Canyon. Pilot died in crash. Parts remain at site.

6/2/73. *Lightplane* crashed at 4,100' level of Whitaker Peak four miles west of Interstate 5. The pilot died in this weather-related crash. Wreck has been removed.

3/14/74. *Cessna 150* crashed on Big Pine Mountain, seriously injuring the

Patric J. Macha examining outer wing of B24E #42-7180 at San Miguel Island. (G.P. Macha) Region 9.

pilot. Aircraft is intact and may have been removed. Weather was a factor in this crash.

9/25/74. *Mooney Mk. 21 N67217U* crashed in Sierra Madre Mountains SE of Timber Peak.

3/6/75. *DeHavilland Twin Otter N42245* carrying US mail crashed in Santa Ynez Mountains near Noon Peak, killing the pilot. Weather was a factor in this accident.

Date unknown. *Beechcraft 36 N288BH* is wrecked in Santa Ynez Mountains north slope. Site is south of Santa Ynez Airport.

Date unknown. *Fairchild C-119G fire-fighting aircraft* crashed in canyon NW of Frazier Park near Cherry Creek. Wreck is visible and unmarked.

4/22/75. *Cessna 310* hit Santa Ynez Peak in bad weather, killing all three persons on board. Wreckage is mostly removed.

5/8/75. *Cessna 337 N333WG* crashed and burned near Mt. Pinos, ten miles west of Gorman, killing both people on board. Wreck site is at 4,500' level. Weather was a factor in this accident.

8/16/75. *Cessna 182 N1222G* crashed and burned while on photo flight near Sespe Hot Springs. One person died, one was seriously injured, and two escaped with minor injuries. Wreck was mostly removed.

2/14/76. *Piper Cherokee N15660* crashed in bad weather five miles north of Fillmore near Sespe Wild Area. All three persons on board died. Status of wreck not known.

2/15/76. *Sailplane* hit Santa Ynez Peak, injuring the pilot. Wreck is removed.

3/3/76. LTV A-7 US Navy crashed west of Wheeler Ridge in Pleito Hills. No other data available.

9/20/76. *Cessna 182 N91620* on south slope of Condor Peak NW of Santa Barbara.

9/6/77. *Piper N2117Y* lies wrecked near Frazier Mountain.

1/1/78. *Cessna 150* crashed in Sisar Canyon north of Santa Paula in

Topatopa Mountains. Both persons on board perished in this weather-related crash. Status of wreck unknown.

2/15/78. *Lightplane* (twin engine) crashed on Frazier Peak in bad weather with only minor injuries for the three people on board. Wreck is removed.

2/28/78. *Rockwell 685* crashed in Santa Ynez Mountains, killing all seven persons on board. Site is 20 miles NW of Santa Barbara and is mostly removed. Weather was a factor in this crash.

3/12/78. *Piper Cherokee* crashed in bad weather 16 miles west of Gorman at 5,500' level, killing two persons and seriously injuring one. Wreck is removed.

10/13/79. *Cessna* crashed in mountains north of Ojai in bad weather, killing both people on board. No other data available.

11/19/79. *Lightplane* hit Big Pine Mountain in bad weather, killing the pilot. Wreck is removed.

3/25/80. *Pitts Special* crashed near Frazier Park in bad weather, killing the pilot. Wreckage is removed.

4/20/80. *Piper Commanche* crashed west of Grapevine near Tecuya Creek in bad weather, killing all four persons on board. Wreckage is mostly removed.

Date unknown. *Piper Aztec N63780* wrecked in mountains east of Santa Maria near Colson Canyon.

11/20/80. *Cessna 172 N5259J* hit mountains near Lake Piru 10 miles NE of Fillmore in cloudy weather, killing the pilot. Wreckage is unmarked and still visible.

Date unknown. *Piper PA-24 N6674P* crashed west of Lebec near Interstate 5. No other data available.

3/22/81. *Cessna 172* crashed in storm 2.5 miles NE of Frazier Park, killing two persons and seriously injuring two others. Wreck is removed.

4/20/81. *Cessna 177 N147BC* in mountains near Frazier Park.

3/8/82. *Piper PA-28 N7497J* lies wrecked and unmarked NE, of Carpinteria in Santa Ynez Mountains.

6/5/82. *Cessna 172* crashed and burned in Santa Ynez Mountains NE of Carpinteria. Accident occurred in cloudy weather and both people on board were killed. Some parts visible at site.

1/21/83. *Cessna 210 N6188N* crashed in Santa Ynez Mountains NW of Santa Barbara.

1/24/83. *Cessna 152 N25061* crashed in mountains ten miles NW of Castaic.

7/21/84. *Piper Cherokee Six N8019N* crashed in Santa Ynez Mountains near Monte Arido NE of Santa Barbara following an in-flight malfunction. All three persons on board perished. Wreck is removed.

7/28/87. A *Bell Textron UH-1N US Navy Antarctic Squadron* crashed in mountains five miles north of Ojai, killing all four men on board. Cause of this accident is not known. Wreck is removed.

9/7/87. *Cessna* crashed near Frazier Park. No other data available.

1/22/88. *Helicopter* hit power lines in Santa Ynez Mountains near former President Reagan's ranch. Both persons on board were killed. Wreck was consumed by post-impact fire.

3/1/88. *Grumman American Yankee N74236* hit Frazier Mountain in bad weather. Wreck is removed.

4/16/88. *Cessna 210* crashed and burned in rugged mountain country 20 miles west of Gorman. Both persons on board were killed. Status of wreck is unknown.

5/18/88. *Beechcraft Bonanza N3322V* crashed in cloudy weather north of Fillmore in Bear Heaven. All four people on board died in the crash.

10/88. Lightplane crashed into low hills five miles SE of Santa Maria Airport, killing all three people on board. Wreck is removed.

2/4/89. *Lightplane* crashed in Santa Ynez Mountains during rain storm. The pilot survived with only minor injuries. Wreck is removed.

9/19/89. *Cessna 310* with two men on board enroute from Reno, Nevada, to Torrance, California, crashed on Pine Mountain Ridge near Reyes Peak in Ventura County. The wreck is scattered at 7,300' level on the north slope of ridge. The weather conditions were poor at the time of this fatal accident.

4/12/90. *Cessna 172 N39155* is wrecked in Topatopa Mountains on SW slope of Topatopa Peak.

1990. *Enstrom Helicopter* force landed NW on side of Hines Peak. No injuries, and helicopter is removed.

7/19/90. *LTV TA-7C US Navy* crashed and burned in the Los Padres National Forest six miles north of Santa Barbara. Both crewmen ejected safely following in-flight malfunction. The wreck is burned, scattered, and partly removed.

5/7/91. *Cessna 140 N89828* on Pine Mountain Ridge north of Rose Valley.

2/7/93. Cessna 172 N79411 crashed in snowstorm, killing all three persons on board. Site is south of Gorman and west of Interstate 5.

Cessna 180 N3151C crashed and burned killing two men and injuring two others on 6/13/66. Wreck is located in Wellman Canyon in the rugged Sierra Madre Mountains of Ventura County. (G.P. Macha Collection)Region 10.

Dan Hammer and a Wright R-1820-49 engine from North American O-47 on the desert near the town of Rice. (D. Hammer) Region 5.

Scattered aircraft debris from a Y1B-17 accident site. (G.P. Macha) Region 4.

Region 11

Region 11 is the Tehachapi Mountains and associated foothills. Some geographers include a portion of the southern High Sierra as part of this region but I have chosen to cover only the Tehachapi Mountains. This area is bordered by Highway 14 on the east, Highway 138 on the south, Interstate 5 on the west, and Highway 58 provides the northern limits. 7,988' Double Mountain is the highest point in this region where locked gates and no trespassing signs abound. More than fifty crash sites are located in these mostly barren mountains of occasional oak and pine forest.

3/20/42. *Vultee BT-13 USAAC* crashed into Castaic Lake two miles east of Lebec. The body of the pilot was recovered on 4/8/42. This aircraft was one of five BTs that disappeared while on a training mission from Minter Field near Bakersfield. Status of wreck is not known.

3/20/42. *Vultee BT-13A #41-1564 USAAF* crashed in bad weather east of Cummings Mountain near Oak Creek. The pilot died along with four other airmen all lost while flying BTs out of Minter Field on what was supposed to have been a routine training mission. Wreck is marked and visible.

3/20/42. *Vultee BT-13 USAAF* crashed north of Cummings Mountain in bad weather, killing the pilot. Wreck is burned and unmarked.

Date unknown. *Beechcraft AT-10 #42-3512 USAAF* lies scattered and unmarked north of the Libre Twins near Cottonwood Creek. No other data.

Date unknown. *Cessna UC-78A #42-8831 USAAF* is burned and unmarked SW of Covington Mountain near Twin Lakes.

10/30/42. *Douglas A-20 USAAF* is marked and was visible on Tehachapi Peak. Aircraft went down in snowstorm en route from Hamilton Field to March Field, killing all three men on board. Wreck was removed in 1970s.

Date unknown. *Beechcraft Staggerwing* is unmarked south of Covington Mountain near White Oak Lodge. No other data available.

12/1/43. *Lockheed C-60 USAAF* crashed in a storm on Bear Mountain, killing all nine men on board. Status of wreck is not known. No other data.

Date unknown. *Piper Pacer NC7569H* crashed NE of Gorman near Pumpkin Peak.

Date unknown. *Vought F4U US Navy* lies scattered and unmarked east of Wheeler Ridge in Tejon Hills. No other data available.

Date unknown. *Aeronca NC-1879E* is burned and unmarked NE of Lebec near California Aqueduct. No other data available.

3/4/53. *Globe Swift N2370* crashed in bad weather near Libre Twins, killing pilot. Status of wreck today is unknown.

2/1/59. *Beechcraft Bonanza N5407D* crashed in bad weather 35 miles east of Bakersfield in Bear Valley. Pilot died in crash and wreck was removed.

12/1/60. Beechcraft Bonanza N9720R was lost with four persons on board while flying over Tehachapi Mountains in winter storm.

8/24/61. *Crash site* is on Bidart Ranch. No other data available.

2/11/62. *Beechcraft Bonanza N2806V* lies intact and marked SE of town of Tehachapi near Covington Mountain. No other data available.

2/25/62. *Beechcraft Bonanza N4499V* hit Bear Mountain in storm, killing all four persons on board. Wreck was not located until 3/19/62. Wreck is unmarked and visible.

12/7/62. *Kaman HH-43B USAF* crashed while on rescue mission south of White Oak Lodge. Weather was a factor in accident and wreck has been removed.

4/2/63. *Piper Tri-Pacer* hit Cummings Mountain in cloudy weather, killing one person and injuring two others. Wreck is unmarked and visible.

8/17/63. *Lightplane* crashed in Cameron Canyon 14 miles SE of town of Tehachapi, seriously injuring both persons on board. Pilot error was listed as a factor in this accident. Status of wreckage is not known.

11/3/64. *Stinson Voyager* crashed at 6,400' level of Bear Mountain in bad weather and all three people on board survived with only minor injuries. Wreck is mostly removed.

Date unknown. *Globe Swift N3818K* crashed in Tehachapi Mountains on private ranch land. Wreck is completely removed. No other data available.

Date unknown. *Beechcraft 35* crashed south of Cummings Valley. Wreck is unmarked.

3/15/65. *Beechcraft 33 N840R* crashed NE of Gorman in Oso Canyon. Status of wreck is unknown.

1/22/69. *US Army helicopter* crashed on delivery flight ten miles west of Tehachapi town center near Bear Mountain. The pilot died in this weather-related accident. Wreck is removed.

1/28/69. *Cessna 172 N7285T* hit mountain eight miles west of town of Tehachapi in bad weather, killing all three persons on board. The wreck is mostly removed.

3/3/69. *Cessna 172 N3798U* hit the 7,500' level of Cummings Mountain in bad weather, injuring both people on board. Wreck is removed.

6/12/69. *Piper Aztec* hit ridge east of Lebec near Interstate 5 in bad weather, killing all three people on board. Wreck is removed.

3/10/70. *Piper Cherokee N8057N* hit mountain near town of Tehachapi. No other data available.

5/3/70. *Sailplane* crashed near Libre Twins. Wreckage is visible at site but no other data is available.

7/29/70. *Grumman TBM* crashed in mountains west of town of Tehachapi while on fire-fighting mission. The pilot was killed and most of the wreckage has been removed.

11/30/71. *Cessna 150* crashed at 4,000' level ten miles north of Gorman, killing the pilot. Weather was a factor in this accident. Status of wreck is unknown.

1/22/72. *Mooney Mk. 20 N6768V* crashed 11 miles south of town of Tehachapi, killing both people on board. Bad weather was a factor in this accident. Wreck is removed.

11/12/72. *Piper Super Cub N8325P* crashed in bad weather NE of Gorman on Tejon Ranch. One person was killed and another was seriously injured. Wreck is removed.

11/30/73. *Beechcraft Muskeeter* hit Sandberg Peak 12 miles north of Gorman, killing all three people on board. No other data available.

11/21/74. *Beechcraft Muskeeter N8340Q* crashed and burned on the NE slope of Bear Mountain. Pilot died in this weather-related accident. Wreck status unknown.

10/29/75. *Alon Aircoupe* crashed at 1,300' level of El Tejon Mountains 35 miles SE of Bakersfield. Both persons on board perished in this weather-related crash. Wreck is removed.

3/30/78. *Piper Twin Commanche N400EW* hit south slope of Bear Mountain in bad weather, killing all three people on board. Wreck is removed.

1/79. *Lightplane* crashed on Blue Ridge Mountain at 6,500' level twenty miles SW of Tehachapi. Pilot died in this weather related crash. Status of wreck not known.

4/28/79. *Cessna 172* hit Grapevine Peak in bad weather, killing two and seriously injuring two others. Site is located east of Interstate 5 and is removed.

Globe Swift N3818K crashed on ranch in the Tehachapi Mountains seriously injuring the pilot. Crash date is late 1960s. (NTSB) Region 11.

12/21/79. *Cessna 172 N6714H* hit ridge north of Gorman because of clear air turbulence. Wreck is intact but all five persons on board were killed in crash. Wreck is still visible as of 4/85.

2/3/80. *Lightplane* crashed half mile east of Wheeler Ridge in bad weather, killing the pilot. Wreck has been removed.

5/20/81. *Lightplane* crashed south of town of Tehachapi in mountains, killing three persons and seriously injuring one. Weather was a factor in this accident. Wreck is removed.

10/16/81. *Cessna 1500 N67926* lies wrecked in Tejon Hills east of Mettler.

10/21/81. *Piper Cherokee* crashed and burned in bad weather SW of town of Tehachapi. Three persons died in this accident.

2/6/83. *Lightplane* crashed at 4,000' level near Fort Tejon, killing all four people on board. Weather was a factor in this accident.

3/1/84. *Cessna 172 N880LS* is wrecked north of Pumpkin Peak.

6/7/84. *Cessna 152 N5335M* crashed in Tehachapi Mountain foothills, killing both people on board. Site is 20 miles west of Rosamond. Weather was a factor in this accident. Status of wreck is unknown.

11/23/84. *Lightplane* crashed in high winds next to Highway 58 in Tehachapi Mountains. Two persons died and one survived this accident. Wreck is removed.

12/1/84. *Cessna 152 N49806* crashed during storm near Libre Twins. Wreck located 12/14/84 with two dead on board. Wreck is visible and unmarked.

12/13/84. *Grumman AA-5 N26131* crashed north of Pumpkin Peak.

10/6/85. *Cessna 210* crashed and burned in Tehachapi Mountains on Tejon Ranch. All four persons on board died in this weather-related accident. Status of wreck is unknown.

11/17/86. *Cessna 150* hit Lookout Peak at 8,000' level, killing both people on board. Wreck is reported removed.

Date unknown. *Beechcraft 35 N9720R* lies wrecked and marked NE of Lebec in upper Tunis Creek.

Date unknown. *Bellanca 300* SW of Double Mountain. Status unknown.

Date unknown. *Cessna 340 N33020* is wrecked north of Pumpkin Peak.

12/26/86. A *Piper Cherokee* crashed ten miles east of Gorman, killing one person and injuring another. Cause of crash is listed as pilot error. Status of wreck is unknown.

5/22/87. *Northrop T-38A #62-3639 USAF* collided with Cessna 206 near town of Tehachapi. Three died and one survived this rare mid-air. Wrecks have been removed.

11/25/88. *Cessna 182 N5545W* crashed in storm north of Pumpkin Peak.

9/29/89. *Cessna 150* crashed in Tehachapi Mountains during the testing of new instrument technology. Both persons on board were killed. Cause of accident is not available at time of writing. Wreck is removed.

4/22/91. *Beechcraft 35 N21760* crashed NW of Mojave in foothills. Wreck is removed.

1/96. *Cessna 210* crashed in mountains east of Gorman during storm, killing both men on board.

Region 12

Region 12 includes Death Valley National Monument, the Panamint Mountains, several lesser ranges, and the White Mountains which dominate the area with 14,246' White Mountain. This region is bounded on the east by the Nevada Border, on the south by the San Bernardino County line, and on the west and north by Highways 395 and 6. This region is characterized by rugged, barren, desert mountains of high summer temperatures and cold winter winds. In this mostly forbidding region lie the remains of about forty aircraft.

8/1/44. A *Consolidated B-24J #42-78532* and *B-24E #42-72862 USAAF* collided at 20,000' raining debris five miles SE of Furnace Creek and killing eighteen men. Scattered, unmarked wreckage is still visible today.

1944-45. *Goodyear FG1 US Navy* was lost during World War II and was not located until 1967. Wreck found by hikers near Saratoga Springs, 35 miles SE of Furnace Creek. Human remains and machine guns were recovered from the crash site in Death Valley National Monument.

Date unknown. *Cessna UC-78 USAAF* is wrecked and unmarked in the Inyo Mountains just east of Keynot Peak. No other information is available.

10/20/44. *Consolidated B-24J 42-41444 USAAF* was visible and marked in Saline Valley east of Lone Pine. Today most of the wreckage has been removed and no marked parts remain. This aircraft went down following the failure of two engines. The pilot made a wheels-down emergency landing in which one crewman was seriously injured and died later that same day.

9/1945. *Grumman F6F-5 #71033 US Navy* crashed south of Tucki Mountain west of Furnace Creek, on Pinot Peak. Unmarked parts are visible as of 3/93.

9/9/51. *Piper Cub N27839* crashed in Panamint Mountains. The pilot escaped with minor injuries and status of wreck is unknown.

12/19/51. *Pratt Reid* glider broke-up at 45,000' while attempting world's record altitude attempt. Pilot Karl Ovgard was killed and the wreckage is widely scattered 4-6 miles NE of Independence in Inyo Range.

1/24/52. *Grumman SA-16A #51-001 USAF* crashed following engine problems and the successful bailout of the five man crew. The plane continued on auto-pilot until it hit the Paramount Mountains. Wreck is visible and marked near Cottonwood Creek, near Town's Pass, north of Highway 190.

1953. *Luscombe N1389K* crashed while on Civil Air Patrol search mission. Wreck is located in Last Chance Range west of Nevada border. The wreck is silver and orange, unmarked, partly burned and visible as of 1996.

Date unknown. *Boeing QB-17G USAF* crashed in Mountain Spring Canyon near China Lake. Wreck is mostly removed.

9/9/53. *US Navy aircraft* crashed and burned on Owens Dry Lake, killing all three crewmen.

10/22/56. *North American F-100C USAF* crashed in Black Mountains of Death Valley National Monument. Site is north of Coffin Peak on ridge.

8/18/58. North American F-100F USAF lies scattered north of Badwater in the Black Mountains south of Furnace Creek. Site is in Death Valley National Monument on Mt. Perry.

Landing gear with inflated tire from F-4J #158379 found more than a quarter mile from the tail section. (G.P. Macha) Region 12.

8/58. *Cessna L-19E #56-2548 US Army* crashed in bad weather, killing the pilot. Wreck was discovered by a deer hunter below Campito Meadow in Sept. 1959. Wreck is unmarked and partly burned.

1/11/59. *Aeronca N26322* crashed 500' below crest of Westguard Pass in the White Mountains. Both people on board died in this bad weather-related accident. Wreck is removed.

Date unknown. *US Navy* drone aircraft wreckage is located north of Trona in Argus Range. Wreck is unmarked.

Date unknown. *Grumman F6F-6K US Navy* target drone crashed in Panamint Range east of Ballarat. Wreck is visible and unmarked.

5/4/61. *Beechcraft Bonanza N3232V* crashed and burned at the edge of Owens Lake just east of Highway 395. No other data available.

11/4/61. *Cessna 150 N7031X* crashed north of Ballarat in the Panamint Range. No other data available.

12/17/61. *Douglas A-4A #142203 US Navy* crashed south of Funeral Peak in Black Mountains of Death Valley National Monument. Wreck is scattered and unmarked.

9/11/62. *Bell 47* crashed on Blanco Mountain in the White Mountains. Wreck is removed.

5/28/63. *Funk Model B N88156* crashed at 3,000' level of Wildrose Peak west of Furnace Creek. Both men on board survived with minor injuries. Status of wreck is unknown.

2/27/65. *Bell 47G N73998* lies burned on Campito Mountain in White Mountains.

4/17/66. *Piper Cherokee N6415W* lies intact in the White Mountains near Westguard Pass east of Bishop. No other data available.

6/2/68. *Piper Cherokee* is visible and marked in the Coso Mountains east of Olancha.

10/29/68. *Cessna 150 N8080F* crashed east of Furnace Creek in Death Valley, killing one person and seriously injuring another. Engine has been removed, but the rest of wreck is visible and unmarked on Echo Mountain.

Patric J. Macha and wing section of F-4J #158379. The widely scattered distribution of this wreckage suggests a possible mid-air or use as a QF-4 Drone, but markings don't match for drone use. (G.P. Macha) Region 12.

Date unknown. *Sikorsky 35 H-34 US Navy* is wrecked and unmarked in Argus Range west of Argus Peak.

12/9/69. *Beechcraft 35 N669B* crashed at north end of White Mountains near Nevada border on Montgomery Peak.

12/15/69. *Republic F-105 USAF* hit mountain in Death Valley National Monument, killing pilot. Status of wreck and other data is unknown.

12/20/69. *Lockheed SR-71A USAF* crashed near town of Shoshone east of Death Valley. Both crewmen escaped with minor injuries following ejection. Wreck is removed, but small parts are still visible.

7/72. *Cessna 172 N8556B* wreck model not known is located in White Mountains SE of Benton in Rock Canyon. The wreckage is red, white, and visible.

8/26/73. *Cessna 170 N8015A* crashed in bad weather, killing all three persons on board. Accident site is in White Mountains near Nevada border at McFee Creek. Wreck is blue, white, and visible.

1970s. *Lockheed QT-33A US Navy* crashed in Argus Range north of Trona. Wreck is partly intact and unmarked.

3/13/74. *Convair 440 N4819C Sierra Pacific Airlines* crashed at 6,500' level of Redding Canyon nine miles east of Bishop in the White Mountains. All thirty-six people on board died. The aircraft had been chartered by a motion picture company that was working on location in the Mammoth Lakes area. Wreck is burned and tail may still be visible. Crash occurred shortly after take-off from Bishop Airport.

2/12/75. *LTV A-7 US Navy* crashed in Inyo Mountains east of Lone Pine. Wreck is scattered in foothills near Long John Canyon.

11/17/75. *Cessna 172 N8886V* crashed in Saline Mountains SE of Big Pine. No other data available.

6/25/80. *Cessna 150 N1535U* crashed near Corkscrew Peak in Death Valley National Monument. Two persons died in this crash. Wreck is scattered and visible near Highway 90.

McDonnell Douglas F-4J #158379 US Navy widely scattered and unmarked near upper Centennial Flat campground in the Cosco Range. The crash date and cause of this accident is not yet known. (G.P. Macha) Region 12.

9/14/80. *LTV A-7 US Navy* crashed and listed as scattered at 36° 12'N 117° 41'W.

1/7/85. *Beechcraft Bonanza* crashed in bad weather, killing all four persons on board. Wreck is located in mountains of Death Valley National Monument.

5/8/89. Two *McDonnell Douglas F/A-18 US Navy aircraft of Fighter Squadron VX-4* collided near Lone Pine. One plane crashed two miles east of Olancha in an area of sand dunes. The other aircraft crashed and burned in foothills eight miles NE of Independence. One pilot died and one survived as a result of this accident. Both wrecks are mostly removed.

2/23/90. *LTV A-7E US Navy* crashed following in-flight malfunction north of China Lake. Pilot ejected safely. Status of wreck is not known.

Date unknown. *Cessna 310* lies wrecked in draw on Corkscrew Peak in Death Valley National Monument.

6/13/90. *McDonnell Douglas F-4E California Air National Guard* crashed on training flight near Highway 27 between Shoshone and Death Valley

Tail of Cessna L-19E #56-2548 US Army near Campito Meadow in the White Mtns. It disappeared 8/58 and was not located until 9/59. (J. Bishop) Region 12.

Junction. Both crewmen died in crash. Wreck is mostly removed, but scattered debris remains.

7/26/90. Two *McDonnell Douglas F-4G USAF* aircraft collided over Death Valley National Monument eight miles SW of Furnace Creek. Two crewmen died and two survived. Wreckage is widely scattered and is partly removed.

Dates unknown. (3) *McDonnell Douglas F4E USAF, F-4J USN, F-4N USN* lie unmarked, scattered, and visible in the Coso Range near Upper Centennial Flat Campground. The *F-4J #15837* was apparently lost as the result of a mid-air collision. This aircraft is scattered, unburned, and partly intact.

Date unknown. *LTV TA-7C US Navy* crashed in the Panamint Mountains, killing both crewmen. Wreck is scattered and unmarked.

Date unknown. *Ultralight aircraft* is wrecked at 36° 50'N 117° 54'W.

5/7/92. *McDonnell Douglas FA-18 US Navy* crashed in Marble Canyon of the White Mountains, killing the pilot. Site is near Grandview Campground.

5/21/93. *McDonnell Douglas FA-18 US Navy* crashed in the foothills of the Inyo Mountains five miles SE of Independence. Pilot ejected safely and wreck is mostly removed.

Tom Gossett and the wreck of a Scheizer 2-32 sailplane in the bottom of the East Fork of the San Gabriel River Canyon near Vincent's Gap. (P. J. Macha) Region 7.

Douglas DC-3 NC-18645 of Western Airlines hit White Mountain in Ventura County on 11/14/46 in a snowstorm. The wreck is visible from I-5. (S. Griggers) Region 9.

Region 13

Region 13 includes the coast ranges of Central California from Highway 166 on the south to San Pablo Bay, and the Sacramento River on the north. Interstate 5 and the Pacific Ocean provide the eastern and western boundaries, respectively. This area includes the Diablo, Santa Lucia, and Temblor Ranges. The highest point is 5,844' Junipero Serra Peak located in the Los Padres National Forest of Monterey County. Dense chaparral covers most of the coastal slopes, with pine and redwood forests common in the northern coastal portions. The ranges bordering the Central Valley are covered by sparse vegetation, with many parts of southern ranges completely barren. More than one hundred-thirty wrecks are found within this region.

12/17/32. *Boeing 40B* carrying US Mail crashed on crest of Rocky Ridge near Danville, killing the pilot. Accident occurred in bad weather. Wreck is removed from Contra Costa County crash site.

3/26/41. *Curtiss P-40B USAAC* crashed following an in-flight fire from which the pilot successfully escaped by parachute. Crash site is on private mountainous land 18 miles NW of Coalinga. Status of wreck is burned and unmarked. Aircraft was attached to 20th Pursuit Group.

3/23/42. *Boeing B-17E USAAF #41-2654* crashed in mountains NW of Coalinga in bad weather. Wreckage is unmarked at 4,000' level of Diablo Range, west of 5,258' San Benito Mountain. An in-flight fire forced the crew of five to bail out, which everyone did successfully. This wreck is buried, but scattered debris is still visible near the head waters of the San Benito River.

1942 *Lockheed P-38 USAAF* crashed in Diablo Range, east of town of Paicines, SE of Hollister. Wreck is visible and marked at 2,200' level.

Date unknown. *Douglas A-20 USAAF* is located south of Carmel and two miles east of Highway 1 at 2,600' level. Wreck is marked but difficult to see and widely scattered.

Date unknown. *Vultee BT-13 USAAF* crashed in mountains west of Patterson killing both crewman. The wreck is mostly buried and site is on private land.

1945. *North American B-25 USAAF* was lost on a training mission, and was presumed to have crashed in the Pacific Ocean. This aircraft was located 8/14/73 by hikers NE of Point Sur in the rugged Santa Lucia Range. The remains of five crewmen were removed from the site, and wreckage was marked with yellow X's. Wreck is located in Granite Canyon with machine guns still at site in late 1973. Wreck was apparently located prior to 8/14/73 but clean-up job was poor and not all human remains were recovered until 1973.

Date unknown. *Fairchild PT-19* is wrecked and visible at 3,500' level east of Fremont. Site is unmarked.

3/15/45. *Douglas R4D US Navy transport plane* crashed in bad weather in hills near San Carlos, killing 21 men and injuring two others. Wreck is removed.

3/19/45. *Boeing B-29 USAAF* hit Wauhab Ridge 30 miles SE of San Francisco in winter storm. All seven men on board perished. The wreck is mostly removed from the 3,800' level.

1/28/48. *Douglas DC-3 NC-36480* crashed in Diablo Range west of

McDonnell F2H-4 #127614 crashed in Stevens Creek N. of Saratoga in bad weather on 2/22/59. Pilot was killed and wreck was marked. (Jim Rowan) Region 13.

Coalinga, killing all persons on board. Status of the wreck is not known.

8/8/48. *Vultee BT-13 NC-57365* lies marked and visible in the mountains east of Hayward at 2,000' level. No other information is available.

Date unknown. *Aircraft wreckage of 1940s vintage* is located in Temblor Range near town of McKitterick. Site is unmarked.

Date unknown. A *Cessna UC-78 NC-69080* is located in Santa Lucia Range south of Santa Margarita. This wreck is unmarked and burned over, with little remaining at site today.

Date unknown. *Fairchild PT-19 NC-48885* is visible and marked in coastal hills near Point Estero north of Morro Bay.

1/22/49. *North American Navion NC4523K* crashed in bad weather SW of Avenal at 2,300' level. Site is marked in Diablo Range and still visible.

9/15/50. *Grumman F8F US Navy* crashed and burned in Diablo Range SW of Coalinga. The pilot died in this accident which was apparently due to systems malfunction. Wreck is burned and unmarked on private land.

8/23/51. *Douglas DC-6B United Airlines* crashed into Tolman Peak killing all fifty people on board. Site is 1.5 miles east of Decoto. Accident occurred at night with low clouds a factor. Some unmarked parts are reported visible today.

Date unknown. *Aeronca NC-31994* is wrecked and unmarked in low hills NE of San Luis Obispo at 2,100' level. Accident was weather-related.

Date unknown. *Luscombe Model 8E* is located in hills NE of town of Arroyo Grande. Wreck may be removed.

4/7/52. *Douglas R4D US Navy* hit Loma Prieta Peak in bad weather, killing all four men on board. Unmarked parts remain at crash site.

3/21/53. *Douglas DC-4 of Transocean Airlines* hit a hill near Decoto killing all thirty-five persons on board. Site is in Alameda County and wreck is removed.

5/14/53. *Stinson N9890* is visible and marked near town of San Lucas in Salinas Valley. Site is in low hills east of Highway 101.

1953. *Douglas DC-3* is reported wrecked and scattered at 37° 15'N and 121°46'W. No other data available.

Date unknown. *Fairchild PT-19 NC-6908* near San Carlos in hills. Wreck may be removed.

Date unknown. *Beechcraft 18* crashed on Mt. Hamilton in Santa Clara County. Some small parts are reported visible at the site which is one mile below summit.

2/17/53. *USAF aircraft* is located in hills east of Fremont in Alameda County. Wreck is unmarked with few parts remaining at site.

10/28/53. *Douglas DC-6 VH-BPE of British Commonwealth Pacific Airlines* crashed enroute from Sydney, Australia to San Francisco, CA. only minutes from its final destination. The crash site is on a heavily wooded 2,000' ridge west of Redwood City on the southwest side of Kings Mountain. The crew of eight and all eleven passengers died in this weather related accident.

11/23/54. *North American F-86D #52-3766 USAF* crashed in Santa Cruz Mountains east of Heckler Pass. Wreck is scattered and unmarked.

Date unknown. *Stinson L-5 N67140* crashed in Diablo Range west of town of Avenal. Parts are still visible at site.

1/18/55. *Douglas AD-6 #134527 US Navy* crashed north of Mt. Hamilton in Santa Clara County. Pilot died in this weather-related accident. Wreck is removed.

2/17/55. *North American T-28A #51-7602 USAF* crashed in bad weather in hills of Alameda County NW of Hayward. Wreck is mostly removed.

Date unknown. *Lockheed L1049H #N6915C* crashed in bad weather on Sweeney Ridge near San Bruno. Unmarked parts reported at site.

4/14/55. *Lockheed TV-2 (T-33B) #138055 US Navy* crashed in Santa Cruz Mountains in bad weather. Wreck is marked but hard to see at 2,900' level NE of Boulder Creek.

2/17/56. *Douglas R5D-1 #39116 USMC* hit low mountains SE of Hayward in Alameda County. Wreck is in Paldmares Canyon, 3.5 miles NE of Niles, and few parts remain at 2,000' level impact site. Forty men died in this weather related accident.

10/5/56. *Stinson N9099K* is visible and marked in Diablo Range east of Mt. Stakes in Stanislaus County. Wreck is yellow and marked with red X's.

10/7/56. *Lockheed TV-2 (T-33B) #138060* crashed in Santa Cruz Mountains of Santa Clara County south of New Almaden. Wreck is scattered and unmarked on Loma Prieta Peak.

10/29/56. *McDonnell F4H-2B #125651 US Navy* hit mountains south of Highway 84 at 2,000' level, killing the pilot. Wreck is unmarked and few parts remain.

10/30/56. *Grumman F9F-6 #12758 US Navy* crashed in hills near Orinda killing pilot. Wreck is unmarked and scattered.

1/7/57. *Stinson N6205M* crashed in bad weather in Santa Cruz Mountains at 3,000' level west of Morgan Hill in Santa Clara County. Wreck is unmarked.

1/27/57. *Ercoupe N32288* crashed in coastal hills south of Half Moon Bay in San Mateo County. Status of wreckage is unknown.

3/4/57. *Cessna 182 N5961B* crashed in storm east of Watsonville in low hills. Wreck is scattered and mostly removed.

8/2/57. *Stearman PT-17 NC-57228* crashed south of town of Jolon on Hunter-Ligget Military Reservation in Monterey County. Wreck is unmarked.

2/22/59. *McDonnell F2H-4 #127614 US Navy Reserve* crashed in hills NW of Saratoga in Santa Clara County. Wreck is unmarked and only a few parts remain.

3/24/59. Two *Chance Vought F8U-1s #14448 and #144451* collided in mid-air NE of Mt. Hamiliton in the Diablo Range of Santa Clara County. Wreckage is widely scattered and mostly removed.

10/26/59. *North American FJ-3 #135978 US Navy* crashed in the mountains near Orinda in Contra Costa County. The wreck is scattered and unmarked. No other data is available.

9/25/60. *Fairchild PT-19 NC-69086* crashed in mountains west of Redwood City in San Mateo County. Status of wreck today is unknown.

9/29/60. *Piper Commanche N6374P* crashed in Santa Lucia Range south of Carmel. No other data is available.

Date unknown. *Ryan Navion* lies marked and visible in mountains south of Coalinga in Fresno County.

Date unknown. *Cessna N5714N* crashed in mountains west of Paso Robles. Wreck is reported marked and visible.

Date unknown. *Grumman F9F-8 US Navy* crashed and burned in La Panza Mountains east of San Luis Obispo. Scattered unmarked wreckage remains at crash site.

11/18/60. *Beechcraft T-34A N5507V* crashed in bad weather at 3,100' level of La Panza Range NE of Santa Maria.

4/11/61. *Douglas AD-5Q #134988 US Navy* crashed and burned near Lake San Antonio in Santa Lucia Range at 2,500' level. Wreck is removed.

6/19/61. *Grumman F9F-8T #146381 US Navy* disappeared on a training flight from Moffett Field with two men on board. The wreck was found by hikers many years later in the Santa Cruz Mountains. Wreck is unmarked and scattered.

7/2/61. *Cessna 170 N3191A* crashed in mountains due south of Salinas. Wreck is reported removed.

Date unknown. *Douglas A-3A US Navy* reported visible, scattered and unmarked at 37° 16'N and 120° 55'W.

Date unknown. *Douglas C-47 USAF* north of Gilroy Hot Springs at 3,000' level. Wreck is marked and visible.

10/7/61. *McDonnell F3H-2 US Navy* crashed in Santa Cruz Mountains near Ben Lomond in Redwood State Park. Wreck is marked and overgrown.

Date unknown. L*ockheed T2V-1 US Navy* crashed in Santa Cruz Mountains near Saratoga. Wreck is scattered and unmarked.

11/20/61. *Cessna 172 N7815T* hit Bald Mountain west of Coalinga, killing both persons on board. Crash occurred in bad weather. Wreck is at 4,000' level and is not marked.

5/27/62. *Waco N17725* crashed in Diablo Range north of Mt. Hamilton. Wreck is unmarked and may be removed.

1/11/63. *Beechcraft Bonanza N4560D* crashed in mountains west of Danville in Contra Costa County. Wreck is unmarked and upside down.

2/16/63. *Cessna 205 N1872F* crashed in hills east of Livermore in Alameda County. Wreck is reported removed.

9/7/63. A *Cessna 172 N8042B* crashed near Redwood City at bottom of San Vincente Canyon. The site is at Moss Beach and some parts remain. Four persons died in crash.

11/16/63. *Mooney Mk. 20 N8318E* crashed in Santa Cruz Mountains NW of

Lockheed TV-2 #138060

On 10/7/56 a Lockheed TV-2 (T-33B) #138060 crashed on Loma Prieta Peak killing the pilot. Scattered unmarked parts like this main landing gear leg still litter the crash site. (Jim Rowan) Region 13.

Gilroy. The wreck is unmarked and scattered. Weather was a factor in this accident.

1/10/64 McDonnell F-101B USAF crashed and burned SW of Danville in coastal hills. Wreck is removed.

1/14/64. A *Cessna 150 N7294X* crashed in bad weather SE of San Jose, seriously injuring the pilot. Site is at 2,000' level of the Diablo Range. Wreck is removed.

2/29/64. *Piper Apache N3186P* crashed in bad weather near Idria in the Diablo Range, killing the pilot. Status of wreck not known.

5/7/64. *Fokker F-27 N2770R* of Pacific Airlines crashed while en route from Stockton to Oakland as a result of gunfire within the cockpit. All forty-four persons perished in this tragic crash. Wreck is mostly removed from hill country near Mt. Diablo.

12/11/64. *Cessna 182 N57045* crashed during a storm in the Diablo Range west of Mendota. Wreck is upside down and unmarked.

12/23/64. *Cessna 120* crashed NE of Morgan Hill in the Diablo Range. Wreck is unmarked, scattered, and hard to see.

Date unknown. *PA-28 N8162P* reported at 37° 03'N and 120° 33'W. Wreck is unmarked.

12/27/64. *Cessna 182 N3187S* crashed in bad weather 17 miles NW of Santa Cruz in Big Basin State Park. All five people on board died in this accident.

1/11/65. *Lockheed T-33B #141506 US Navy* crashed in bad weather in hills east of Fremont. Wreck is scattered and mostly removed.

2/27/65. *Cessna 140 N1154Y* crashed in Browns Canyon 30 miles east of Arroyo Grande. Wreck is scattered and visible. Pilot died in this weather-related accident.

7/8/65. *Waco biplane* is listed wrecked and burned at 37° 23'N 121° 21'W.

7/8/65. *Douglas A-4 US Navy* crashed and burned in the Diablo Range SW of town of Patterson. Status of the wreck is unknown. The pilot did make a successful bailout and was not injured.

10/15/65. *Douglas A-4 US Navy* unmarked and scattered at 36° 22'N 120° 22'W.

Date unknown. *Piper Colt* crashed at Cuesta Summit north of San Luis Obispo, killing all four men on board. Wreck is burned and removed. Weather was a factor in this accident.

3/27/66. *Cessna 150 N6423T* crashed near Mt. Hamilton in Diablo Range. Accident occurred in bad weather, pilot was killed. Wreck is mostly removed.

5/28/66. *Beechcraft Bonanza N5190C* crashed ten miles NE of San Luis Obispo in cloudy weather, killing both persons on board. Status of wreck is unknown.

8/4/67. *Cessna 150 N43C9U* crashed in mountains near Morgan Hill. Both persons on board were seriously injured in the accident, and wreck was removed.

8/8/67. *Grumman HU-16E #2128 USCG* crashed while on search mission north of San Luis Obispo near Highway 1. Heavy fog was a factor in this accident that killed three, and seriously injured five other crewmen. All wreckage was removed from the crash site in low coastal hills.

1/29/68. *Piper Commanche* hit Isabella Peak 15 miles south of San Jose. Crash site is at 4,000' level, and is mostly removed. Weather was a factor in this accident that killed one man.

2/16/68. *Sikorsky CH-53 USMC* hit mountain 40 miles south of San Jose, killing all six men on board. Wreck is removed. Weather was a factor in this crash.

5/68. A *Beechcraft Bonanza N877T* hit hills NE of Berkeley in cloudy weather. One person died and wreck is removed.

6/1/68. *Piper Apache N3186* crashed in Diablo Range near New Idria. No other data available.

8/1/68. *Piper Tri-Pacer N5731P* crashed in Gabilan Range east of Salinas. No other data available.

9/1/68. *Lightplane* crashed on mountain near Carmel Valley Airport, injuring all three people on board. Wreck was removed.

9/68. *Piper Cherokee N4593J* crashed in cloudy weather in foothills east of Salinas, killing four adults and two children. Wreck is removed.

11/21/68. *Beechcraft Bonanza* crashed in Diablo Range east of Morgan Hill, killing three people on board. Weather was a factor in this accident. Wreck was mostly removed.

12/2/68. *Cessna 170 N49F* disappeared on a flight from Lodi to Santa Monica with three people on board. Wreck was located nine miles NE of San Luis Obispo on 1/4/71. All had perished in this weather-related accident. Wreck is marked and visible.

1/18/69. *Mooney Mk. 21 N59037Q* crashed in bad weather west of Pleasanton in mountains, killing both persons on board. Wreck is unmarked and mostly removed.

2/3/69. *Cessna 150 N50378* crashed in mountains near Big Sur with only minor injuries to both people on board. Wreck is removed.

7/28/69. *Cessna 150 N6416F* crashed in mountains north of Gilroy Hot Springs. No other data available.

Wing section from Douglas DC-6 VP-BPE of British Commonwealth Airlines crashed in foggy weather on 10/28/53 killing all nineteen persons on board. Site is near Skeggs Point in San Mateo County. (Jim Rowan) Region 13.

8/17/69. *Piper Cherokee N9695W* crashed in cloudy weather in Perfumo Canyon ten miles east of San Luis Obispo. Both people on board perished in this accident. Wreck is unmarked and mostly removed.

12/10/69. *Beechcraft Travelaire N8619M* crashed in bad weather in Santa Lucia Range north of Cape San Martin. Wreck is scattered and visible.

Date unknown. *Grumman F9F-8 US Navy* target drone is scattered in Los Padres National Forest, San Luis Obispo County. No other data available.

5/26/70. *Piper Cherokee N5706F* crashed in cloudy weather in mountains south of Salinas. Scattered wreckage is visible today.

8/70. *Aeronca N9384E* crashed east of Mt. Hamilton in Diablo Range. Wreck is removed.

11/9/70. *Lockheed T-1A #144302 US Navy* crashed in bad weather SE of Big Sur, killing both men on board. Wreck is visible, grey and scattered.

Date unknown. *Cessna 172 N733HG* reported wrecked in mountains SW of Tracy.

12/1/70. *Lightplane* disappeared with two persons on board. Wreck was found at Cuesta Pass in heavy brush on 5/4/71. Weather was a factor in this accident. Wreck is removed.

12/29/70. *McDonnell Douglas A-4E USMC* hit ridge west of Crystal Reservoir near Burlingame. Pilot safely ejected. Wreck is removed.

4/9/71. *Cessna 185* crashed in cloudy weather in the Orinda Hills of Contra Costa County. All persons on board survived with injuries and wreck is removed.

10/71. *North American T-6G N3437G* crashed in bad weather near Cantu Creek in Diablo Range east of Soledad. Pilot was killed and wreck is visible but not marked. Aircraft had disappeared en route from El Monte to Hayward. Wreck was not located until 1/1/72.

11/12/71. *Piper Cherokee N3626R* crashed in bad weather near Cuesta Summit, north of San Luis Obispo, killing all three persons on board. Wreck is removed.

8/4/72. *McDonnell Douglas A-4F USMC* crashed 15 miles SW of Avenal in

Diablo Range. The pilot ejected following systems malfunction. Wreck is scattered and burned.

10/9/72. *Cessna 172* hit 3,800' Loma Prieta Mountain 20 miles SE of Los Gatos. All three persons escaped with minor injuries in this weather-related accident. Wreck is removed.

12/22/72. *Twin engine lightplane* hit low hills east of Oakland in very bad weather, killing both people on board. Wreck is removed.

3/25/73. *Piper Cherokee N9250W* crashed in bad weather west of Cedar Mountain in Alameda County. Wreck is visible and unmarked.

3/21/73. *NA-1 N2366T* crashed in mountains north of Santa Cruz. No other data available.

5/15/73. *Sikorsky S-58* crashed east of Carmel Valley in mountains at 2,000' level. No other data available.

3/29/74. *Cessna 172 N46041* hit ridge near Pacheco Pass west of Los Banos. Crash occurred in bad weather, killing all on board. Wreck is scattered and visible.

4/8/74. Cessna 172 N5594R crashed in mountains west of Los Banos near San Luis Reservoir. All four persons died in this weather-related accident.

Date unknown. *Beechcraft 35 N3854B* listed wrecked at 37° 10'N 121° 14'W.

Date unknown. *Beechcraft 35 N8571R* reported crashed 37° 20'N 121° 36'W.

2/12/75. *LTV A-7 US Navy* is reported scattered and unmarked at 36° 36'N 121° 01'W.

2/13/75. *Cessna 182 N923M* lies visible and unmarked in mountains west of Gustine and north of San Luis Reservoir. Weather was a factor in this crash.

10/7/75. *Piper Cherokee N4612R* lies wrecked near Mt. Oso west of Patterson. No other data available.

10/27/75. *Beechcraft Model 18 N24594* crashed in mountains NW of Coalinga. Status of wreck today unknown.

5/25/77. *Grumman American Tiger N81003* crashed in cloudy weather, NE of San Luis Obispo near Black Mountain, killing all on board. Status of wreck is not known.

8/21/77. *Piper PA-28 N8474F* hit Mt. Aramat in bad weather, killing all four on board. Site is near Los Banos and is removed.

9/22/77. *Cessna 172 N1786V* is listed at 36° 20'N and 121° 39'W.

12/1/77. *Cessna 150* is wrecked at 37° 05'N and 121° 26'W.

12/12/77. *Piper PA-28 N4754L* is listed at 37° 00'N and 121° 42'W.

2/18/78. *Mooney Mk. 20C* crashed into San Bruno Canyon near Morgan Hill, killing all four persons on board. Wreckage is removed.

3/4/78. *Lightplane* crashed in Hecker Canyon near Mt. Hamilton in bad weather, killing the pilot. Wreck is removed.

9/10/78. *Beechcraft Sierra* crashed in mountains near Big Sur in cloudy weather, killing all four persons on board. Wreck is removed.

2/20/79. *Lightplane* hit Mt. Hamilton near its 4,209' summit, killing both persons on board. Weather was a factor in this crash east of Santa Clara. Wreck is removed.

4/20/80. *Cessna 182* crashed near Cuesta Summit north of San Luis Obispo, killing all five persons on board. Weather was a factor in this accident. Wreck is removed.

4/22/80. *Business jet aircraft* hit Fremont Peak in Gabilan Mountains near Salinas, killing all four on board. Weather was a factor in this accident. Wreck is scattered and partly removed.

11/2/81. *Homebuilt aircraft* is wrecked in hills SE of Livermore. Site is unmarked.

Date unknown. *North American T-28A* civil registration crashed at 36° 48'N and 121° 06'W.

2/13/82. *Cessna 172* hit 3,400' Cathedral Peak 100' below summit in bad weather, killing all four persons on board. Some wreckage remains at site 65 miles south of San Francisco.

2/13/82. *Lightplane* crashed in bad weather in Pacheco Pass west of Los Banos, killing both persons on board. Wreck is removed.

2/13/82. *Beechcraft 23 N6049B* crashed in bad weather in Diablo Range near Gilroy, killing all four on board. Wreck is removed.

1982. *Lightplane* crashed and burned near Morgan Hill, killing all four on board. Wreck was removed.

7/7/83. *Cessna 150 N6599L* visible near Pleasanton in hills.

8/7/83. *Cessna 172 N64196* crashed in mountains south of Monterey in cloudy weather, killing all four on board. Status of wreck is unknown.

2/21/84. *Cessna 182 N91227* is wrecked in low hills east of Fremont.

9/28/84. *Grumman S-2 N436DF* belonging to the California Department of Forestry crashed while on a fire-fighting mission SE of Monterey. Wreck is located on west slope of Mt. Toro. The pilot died in the crash.

10/6/85. Grumman Tiger crashed in cloudy weather in Oakland Hills near Caldicott Tunnel. All three persons on board died in crash. Wreck is removed.

1/31/87. *Cessna 172* crashed in bad weather near Cuyama in San Luis Obispo County, killing both people on board. Crash site was in hills near Highway 166 and wreck is removed.

10/31/87. *Lightplane* crashed in canyon near Mt. Hamilton in Santa Clara County. Both persons on board survived with injuries. Pilot error listed as cause of crash. Wreck is removed.

12/7/87. *British Aerospace 146-200 of Pacific Southwest Airlines* en route from Los Angeles to San Francisco crashed following shooting of flight crew by former airline employee. Aircraft impacted in near vertical dive on hillside north of Morro Bay. All forty-four persons on board died in crash. Aircraft disintegrated on impact. Wreckage is removed.

1/9/88. *Cessna 401* hit ridge in cloudy weather and exploded, killing both persons on board. Crash site is at 1,000' level near Pleasanton. Wreck is removed.

4/2/88. *Lightplane* crashed into a hillside near Orinda in bad weather, killing five persons on board. The wreck was consumed by fire. No other data.

4/16/88. *Cessna 172* hit hills near Los Banos, killing all four on board. This weather-related wreck is removed.

11/17/88. *Cessna 172 N625F* in mountains NE of Fremont at 3,000' level.

5/5/89. *Cessna 152* crashed at night in hills SW of San Luis Obispo Airport, killing both people on board. Wreck is removed.

5/12/89. *McDonnell Douglas F-4G USAF* crashed in mountains of Monterey County near King City. One crewman died and one ejected safely. Wreck is scattered and mostly removed.

Date unknown. *Beechcraft Baron* is listed at 36° 44'N and 121° 29'W.

Date unknown. *Cessna 172 N46401* is listed at 37° 02'N and 121° 12' W.

Date unknown. *Lightplane* is listed at 37° 26'N and 121° 15'W.

Date unknown. *Cessna 172 N4933B* is listed at 37° 30'N and 122° 06'W.

11/25/90. Piper PA-28 N2601X crashed in hills SE of Fremont. Wreck is removed.

6/16/96. *Cessna 152* crashed, killing two men in the rugged Los Padres National Forest in Monterey County. Wreck was not located until 7/18/96.

US Navy personel remove equipment from Douglas A-1E #132435 USN that crashed while searching for a missing TA-4F. Both crewman survived a hard landing near Mt. Whitney at 12,000' level. (R. Koch) Region 14.

Wreck of Curtiss P-40 #39-285 near Roaring River Ranger Station in Sequoia Nat. Park. Lt. Jack C. West bailed out seconds before impact. (P.J. Macha) Region 14.

REGION 14

Region 14 includes the Sierra Nevada Mountains and Cascade Range. This area is bounded on the north by Oregon, on the east by Highway 395 and the Nevada border. The southern boundary is Highway 58, and the western limits are Highway 99 and Interstate 5. Within this region are the highest peaks in all of California including 14,495' Mt. Whitney, highest point in the continental United States. Mt. Shasta at 14,162' is the giant of the volcanic Cascade Range. Here also are vast tracks of wilderness and the resting places for hundreds of aircraft.

2/1/32. *Douglas 0-38 California Air National Guard* crashed in snow storm following pilot and observer bail-out near Oriole Lake in Sequoia National Park. The pilot died, but the observer hiked to safety. The wreck and the pilot's body were not found until April of 1932. The plane had been en route from Griffith Park Airfield, Los Angeles, to Crissy Field, San Francisco. Wreck is unmarked and very hard to find in heavy undergrowth. The engine was removed during the 1950s.

2/3/32. *Boeing Model 40B* carrying US Mail crashed in bad weather near High Sierra town of Rio Vista, killing the pilot. A few burned pieces remain at crash site.

10/3/34. *Martin B-10 USAAC* broke up in flight due to clear air turbulence 50 miles north of town of Bishop. Wreckage is still visible in Dead Man's Gulch. Three crewmen died and one parachuted to safety.

Date unknown. *Ryan B-1* crashed near Tunnel Meadows in the Golden Trout Wilderness. This wreck was removed by Sierra Club in 1974.

1935. *Martin B-10 USAAC* crashed in bad weather near Cahoon Meadow below Silliman Pass. Much of this wreck has been buried, but several hundred pounds of unmarked metal remains visible. Four men perished in this accident when pilot flew too low during filming of squadron in flight and hit trees.

3/1/38. *Douglas DC-2 NC-1299 of Trans World Airlines* en route from San Francisco to Burbank with nine persons on board crashed well off course in the High Sierra. Wreck was not located until 6/12/38. Crash site is on 9,700'

Buena Vista Crest, east of Wawona in Yosemite National Park. All on board perished in this weather-related accident.

10/6/41. *Lightplane* crashed in bad weather at Monache Meadows, killing all three persons on board. Status of this site is not known.

10/24/41. Five *Curtiss P-40 USAAF fighter aircraft of the 57th Pursuit Group* were lost over the High Sierra in bad weather. These P-40s are of the earliest production series and are not B or C models. The armament carried by these aircraft were two .50-caliber and two .30-caliber guns. All of these P-40s were part of a flight of nineteen that was enroute from March Army Base in Riverside County to McClellan AAB in Sacramento County.

Lt. John Pease bailed out of *P-40 #39-213* north of Lake Isabella and his plane crashed in the Kennedy Meadows area of Tulare County. This wreck was reported removed in the mid-40s. Exact location of crash site is unconfirmed. Pilot walked out without injury and was taken by a ranger to Little Lake on Highway 395.

Two pilots bailed out near Barton Peak in Sequoia National Park and managed to find each other on the ground. One of these wrecks lies near Roaring River Ranger Station and the other, *P-40 #39-194* flown by Lt. Lydon, has never been found. The Roaring River wreck is unmarked and was mostly removed during the summer of 1990. Lt. Jack C. West and Lt. Leonard Lydon survived their wilderness experience and were rescued when they were spotted by a B-18 search aircraft after eight days of enduring thebitter cold.

Second Lieutenant Richard N. Long did not bailout and crashed to his death west of South Guard Lake in rugged Cunningham Creek. This site is five miles SE of the Roaring River wreck, but was not located until the summer of 1959. Although the wreck is marked, little was removed until August of 1989.

A memorial statement placed in a metal tube honors 2nd Lt. Long at the 11,200' impact point. A cairn marks his memorial a few feet from *Curtiss P-40 #39-287*.

Farther to the north near Bass Lake another P-40 #39-200 plunged to earth, killing its pilot, Lt. W. H. Birrell. On 5,500' Gray's Mountain lies some unmarked wreckage and a memorial marker honoring the pilot.

In August 1990 a "Project Tomahawk" expedition reached the wreck of Lt.

Jack West's *P-40 #39-285* near Roaring River Ranger Station and removed everything except one propeller blade and parts of the engine block. These remaining parts are now a memorial marker and should not be disturbed.

The search for Lt. L. Lydon's *P-40 #39-194* will continue near Mt. Brewer and the Sphinx Crest until this rare plane is found. The loss of so many fine men and planes rests squarely with the squadron C.O. who ordered his men to fly into the appalling weather system that covered most of California on that fateful October day.

10/24/41. *Douglas B-18 USAAF* crashed while en route to search for the missing P-40s on Sutter Butte north of Yuba City in Yuba County. All five men on board perished in the crash. Wreck is mostly removed from the 1,000' impact area.

10/41. *Stearman PT-17 #41-8091 USAAF* crash-landed two miles north of Balch Camp while searching for missing P-40s, injuring both pilot and observer. Wreck is unmarked, visible and intact.

10/29/41. *Vultee BT-13 USAAF* crashed while participating in the P-40 search flight, killing both men on board. Crash site is unmarked and mostly removed near Balch Camp east of Pine Flat Lake in Fresno County.

11/3/41. *Boeing B-17D USAAF* broke up in flight over 6,000' Tells Peak near the High Sierra community of Georgetown. Severe turbulence was listed as the cause of this crash that killed one man and caused eight others to bail out. Unmarked wreckage remains at this site today.

12/12/41. *Douglas B-18 #36-306 USAAF* en route from Arizona to Hamilton Field north of San Francisco disappeared while flying in snow storm. The aircraft carried a crew of six plus three passengers that included General Herbert A. Dargue. The wreckage was not discovered until 5/8/42 when the father of the copilot found the crash location on Birch Mountain SW of Lone Pine. The wreckage was partly submerged in Kidd Lake, but one wing was intact and visible on the mountainside. A large yellow X painted on this wing remained clearly visible until the Sierra Club removed all of the wreckage in 1973. One unmarked engine was left at the site to serve as a monument. US Army CH-47 helicopters assisted in the recovery effort. Removal of such an historic wreck as a pure salvage exercise raised controversy among aviation enthusiasts at the time.

Date Unknown. *Vultee BT-13 USAAF* crashed in rugged mountains north of town of Tehachapi, killing the pilot. Wreck was discovered by a hunter around 1955-57. Wreck was reasonably intact and the pilot's remains were recovered. No other data available.

11/18/42. *Beechcraft AT-7 #41-21079 USAAF* hit Mt. Darwin in Kings Canyon National Park, killing all four men on board. Wreck was not located until 9/24/47 by a hiker crossing the Mendel Glacier. Attempts to recover bodies proved to be extremely difficult, but a crack US Army mountaineering team is thought to have succeeded in the summer of 1948. Wreck is unmarked and not visible.

12/42. *Vultee BT-13 USAAF* crashed near Sherwin Summit NW of Bishop, killing the pilot. Unmarked parts remain at site today.

3/13/43. *Douglas SBD-4 USN* crashed north of town of Tehachapi, killing the pilot. This aircraft was one of four that had departed Reeve Naval Air Station on Terminal Island, San Pedro, California bound for Seattle, Washington. Only one aircraft reached its destination.

3/13/43. *Douglas SBD-4 #06854* crashed in winter storm north of town of Tehachapi in southern Sierra Nevada. Pilot died in crash. Status of wreck today is not known.

3/13/43. *Douglas SBD-4 #10331* hit Mt. Shasta at 12,000' level, killing both men on board. Crash occurred in bad weather. Wreck is unmarked and buried by snow and ice.

6/21/43. *Consolidated B-24E #42-7118 USAAF* hit Koip Peak NW of June Lake at 12,000' level. All seven men on board were killed in this weather-related training accident. Wreck is scattered and unmarked. This wreck was not located until 6/5/45.

12/5/43. A *Consolidated B-24E #41-2846 USAAF* disappeared while on a routine training flight that originated at Hammer Field near Fresno, California. The wreck was discovered by members of the US Geological Survey on 7/29/60 near Le Conte Mountain at the 12,000' level. Wreckage is scattered down to the 11,000' level. Six men died in this weather-related crash, including 2nd Lt. Robert Hester, the plane's co-pilot for whom a lake at the crash site has been named. Hester's father had spent years searching for his son's plane until his death in 1959. The scattered unmarked wreckage remains visible in Kings Canyon National Park to this day.

Date unknown. *Vultee BT-13 USAAF* crashed following a mid-air collision, killing the pilot. The wreck is scattered and unmarked on Chalk Bluffs seven miles north of Bishop. The other aircraft involved landed safely.

Date unknown. *Vultee BT-13 USAAF* is reported at 39° 27'N and 120° 45'W.

Date unknown. *Boeing B-17 USAAF* crashed NE of Tehachapi near Enault Peak. Most of wreck was removed.

12/6/43. *Consolidated B-24E USAAF* was lost on a training flight from Hammer Field near Fresno. Two crewman bailed out in a snow storm near Huntington Lake in the High Sierra, but six other crewmen and the aircraft itself remained unlocated until Huntington Lake was drained on 9/25/55. The extremely cold lake water preserved the bodies of the crew and the aircraft itself. The pilot had apparently attempted a landing on the frozen lake surface with his bomb bay doors in the open position. Since the lake ice was only a few inches thick, disaster ensued. The wreck was removed from Huntington Lake by a businessman who hoped to charge admission for seeing the reconstructed plane. Status of this operation today is not known.

1943. *Douglas C-47 USAAF* crashed in Parker Pass, killing all persons on board. The weather was a major factor in this accident. The wreck is visible

Douglas AD-6 #139669 USN crashed in the early 1960's near Olmstead View in Yosemite National Park. The pilot died in this accident. (J. Bishop) Region 14.

and unmarked NW of Mammoth Lakes. No other data is available.

1/19/44. Two *Vultee BT-13 USAAF* mid-air twenty-five miles NW of Bishop, east of Highway 395 near Crowley Lake. The other aircraft returned to base.

Date unknown. *Curtiss C-46* crashed and is listed at 39° 12'N and 120° 46'W.

Date unknown. *Vultee BT-13 USAAF* listed as wrecked and marked west of Lake Tahoe at 39° 12'N and 120° 32'W.

4/13/44. *Douglas P-70 #42-5413 USAAF* crashed in bad weather, killing the pilot. Crash site is located east of Wawona, near Givens Creek. Wreck is smashed and unmarked SW of Moraine Mountain.

1944. *North American B-25D #41-30140 USAAF* hit on the west side of 8,320' mountain NW of Lake Isabella. Wreck is marked and visible. The entire crew died in this weather-related accident. Scattered unmarked parts remain on Sunday Peak.

4/44. *Curtiss C-46 USAAF* crashed in bad weather, killing all on board, east of Highway 80 near the town of Weimar in Placer County. Wreck is marked and visible.

8/28/44. *Douglas P-70B USAAF* crashed while on routine training flight at the 11,000' level of Mt. Quarry in Yosemite National Park. Both men on board were killed in this weather-related accident. Plane was from Hammer Field near Fresno. Wreckage is visible and scattered over 500' area.

1944-45. *Boeing B-29BW 45-21843* is marked and scattered NE of Chico at 39° 57'N and 121° 44'W.

1944-45. *Military aircraft* hit 13,157' Mt. Ritter, killing all four men on board. No other data available.

2/2/45. *Curtiss R5C-1 #39584 USMC* hit mountain ridge near Mt. Whitney in a winter storm, killing all seven men on board. Wreck was almost intact, marked, and undisturbed at it's 11,000' resting place until USMC helicopters removed all of the debris at the request of the National Park Service in the summer of 1974.

3/16/45. Douglas C-47 #43-3067 USAAF crashed at 9,000' level near

Tuolumne Meadows on Mt. Lewis in a winter storm, killing all four men on board. Wreck is marked and visible. Wreck was located by deer hunters on 9/23/45.

4/5/45. *Two Stearman PT-17 ex-USAAF* aircraft being ferried from Wickenburg, Arizona, to Portland, Oregon, crashed at 8,000' level in Bishop Creek Canyon near the Old Cardinal Mine, close to Sabrina Lake. Both ex-WASP pilots survived with minor injuries and wrecks were mostly cleaned up in the summer of 1945.

6/23/45. *Douglas C-47 USAAF* crashed in bad weather near Iowa Hill, east of Interstate 80 in Placer County. All on board were killed. Wreckage is reported as still visible at site.

Date unknown. *Vultee BT-13* is reported marked with red X's near Cattle Mountain SE of Madera.

3/21/46. *Douglas C-47 USAAF* crashed in mountains near Truckee in bad weather, killing all twenty-six men on board. Status of this wreck today is not known.

6/6/46. *Stearman PT-17 NC-6454* crashed near Hockett Peak east of Three Rivers in Sequoia National Park. Marked wreckage is said to still be visible at crash site. No other data available.

1946. *Cessna UC-78 NC-5458* crashed near Hockett Peak in Sequoia National Park. Wreck is marked, but no longer visible. Crash is related to PT-17 listed above, but no other details are available.

10/30/46. *Taylorcraft NC-96208* crashed in bad weather on south slope of Mt. Lassen. Extensive search failed initially to locate plane and the two occupants. On 6/11/47 an Army Air Force pilot spotted the wreckage. A ground search team subsequently removed both bodies. Site was marked, but is no longer visible.

Date unknown. *Beechcraft Staggerwing* crashed near Templeton Meadows. Unmarked wreck removed by Sierra Club in 1974.

Date unknown. *Waco cabin biplane* crashed near Tunnel Meadows. Wreck was removed by Sierra Club in 1974.

1/13/47. *Vultee BT-13 NC-62742* crashed in storm NW of Grass Valley. Wreck is marked.

Wreck of B-24E #41-7118 USAAF that crashed on Koip Peak killing all seven crewman. Crash date was 6/21/43. (R. Koch) Region 14.

3/7/47. *Vultee BT-13 NC-58661* crashed in bad weather west of Lake Tahoe, killing the pilot. Wreck is marked and scattered.

5/30/47. *Stinson NC-97999* hit mountain peak west of Nevada City. Wreck is marked. No other data available.

Date unknown. *Vultee BT-13* crashed near Tunnel Meadows Airstrip in the Golden Trout Wilderness. Wreck was removed by Sierra Club in 1974.

11/13/47. *Vultee BT-13 NC-58778* crashed in storm at eastern border of Lassen National Park, in Lassen County. Wreck is marked and visible.

11/47. *Waco NC-17745* flown by famed High Sierra pilot Bob White crashed near south fork of Kern River, near Craig Peak. White survived the crash, but his deer hunter passenger did not. This wreck was slated for a Sierra Club clean-up operation, but the club was asked to hold off until a better date could be arranged. NC-17745 is now situated at Chino Airport awaiting restoration. Powerplant remains at site.

Date unknown. *Vought F4U USMC* hit Kain Peak NE of Tehachapi.

1948. *Lightplane* stalled and crashed at mining site near Kernville, killing both men on board. Monument marks crash site but no wreckage remains.

Date unknown. *Piper J-3* crashed near Bear Trap Meadow in the Golden Trout Wilderness of Tulare County. Wreck removed by Sierra Club in 1974.

12/22/48. *Lightplane* crashed in storm east of Interstate 5 in Shasta County. Wreck is in mountains and is unmarked. No other data is available.

2/3/49. *Beechcraft JRB-4 #90550 US Navy* crashed in storm west of Highway 395 near Owens Peak in Kern County, killing all on board. Wreck is broken up and marked.

Date unknown. *Aeronca Sedan* crashed at Hessian Meadow during attempted landing. Wreck removed by Sierra Club in 1974.

4/6/49. *Beechcraft Bonanza NC-3704N* hit ridge north of Highway 80 in Nevada County, killing all on board. Wreck is marked and visible.

12/16/49. *Vultee BT-13 NC-56865* crashed in Shasta County near Big Bend. Wreck is marked and parts are still visible. Accident occurred in bad weather. No other data available.

12/17/49. *Beechcraft T-11 #41-9564 USAF* crashed in storm east of Grass Valley, killing all on board. Wreck is scattered and unmarked.

3/2/50. *Stinson NC-723?* crashed in bad weather east of Mt. Brewer, SW of Kearsarge Pass. No other data available.

9/18/50. *Cessna 170* crashed in Lassen National Park, NW of Lassen Peak. Wreck is marked. No other data available.

10/25/50. *Vultee BT-13 NC-56639* crashed in bad weather east of Forestville in Placer County. Accident occurred in bad weather and pilot was killed. Wreck is marked and visible.

Date unknown. *Vultee BT-13B* crashed at Hessian Meadow in Golden Trout Wilderness of Tulare County. Wreck removed by Sierra Club in 1974.

10/26/50. *Douglas C-47B #43-49030 USAF* crashed in snow storm while en route from Hill AFB in Utah, to McClellan AFB in California. Wreck was located near Independence Lake, north of Truckee at 9,000' level in the spring of 1951. Wreck is 200' below crest and is unmarked.

Date unknown. *North American F-51D California Air National Guard* crashed in Yosemite National Park following pilot bail-out. Wreck was mostly removed by Sierra Club in the mid-1970s. Wreck location was 38° 04'N and 119° 26'W.

11/18/50. *North American Navion NC-91691* crashed in storm SW of Lake Tahoe in El Dorado County. All on board died in accident. Wreck is marked.

11/20/50. *Cessna N5714C* crashed in storm west of Lassen Peak in Shasta County. Wreck is marked. No other data available.

1/1/51. *Vultee BT-13 N63038* crashed after taking off from Monache Meadows in Tulare County. Wreck was highly visible and unmarked until removed by Sierra Club in 1973. Wreck was at 10,200' level. Wreck site was between summit and Olancha Peaks.

12/26/51. *Douglas C-47A #43-4812 USAF* crashed in snow storm on east slope of Mt. Lassen near Cresent Crater at 7,000' level. Eight men died in this crash that was located by a hiker on 5/25/52. Wreck is visible but unmarked as of 1983. **(For more details see inset Map next page)**

1/29/52. *Chance Vought F4U-4 USMC* crashed near summit of 11,429' Mt. Sonora in bad weather. Pilot survived uninjured and was rescued. Wreck was marked and intact until salvage operations commenced at this site in August of 1991. Tragically the renowned helicopter pilot Rory Rogers was killed on 8/31/91 attempting to remove the F4U engine on his final lift.

2/22/52. *Cessna 170* crash landed in heavy snow 14 miles east of McCloud in Shasta County. Four men on board survived this weather-related accident. Wreck was removed.

8/23/52. *North American SNJ-4 US Navy* crashed south of Kearsarge Pass NW of Lone Pine. Wreck is marked and visible eighteen miles west of Onion Valley. Both crewmen died in this fiery accident.

Date unknown. *Ryan PT-22* crashed at 10,800' level of Mt. Hopkins in Pioneer Basin. Wreck was unmarked and smashed. Sierra Club removed debris in mid-70s.

Date unknown. *Stinson L-5* crashed at Hessian Meadow in the Golden Trout Wilderness. Wreck removed by Sierra Club in 1974.

Date unknown. *Beechcraft Bonanza* crashed one mile SE of Tempelton

Meadow on mountainside. Wreck removed by Sierra Club in 1974. Site is in Golden Trout Wilderness of Tulare County.

Date unknown. *Ercoupe* hit Johnson Peak at 10,000' level, killing both men on board. Site is located in Golden Trout Wilderness of Tulare County. Wreck was removed by Sierra Club in 1974. No other data available.

1950s. *Vultee BT-13* civil registration stalled and crashed shortly after take-off from Monache Meadows airfield, killing the pilot. Wreck was removed by the Sierra Club in the 1970s.

12/26/51. *Douglas C-47A #43-48142 USAF* crashed in a blinding snow storm on the NE side of Lassen Peak just below Cresent Crater at the 7,400' level. Eight men died in this accident that remained undiscovered until a hiker crossing the "devastated area" (from the 1914 eruption) looked up and saw metal reflecting on 5/25/52. It is not uncommon for this wreck to remain snow covered for ten months of the year, so any trip to this site must take the previous winter into consideration. Park your vehicle on Highway 89 (Lassen Park Road) 1.4 miles to the C-47A wreck that shines on the lower mountain in the midday summer sun. You will cross Lost Creek and part of the devastated area before climbing into a partly forested mountain side.

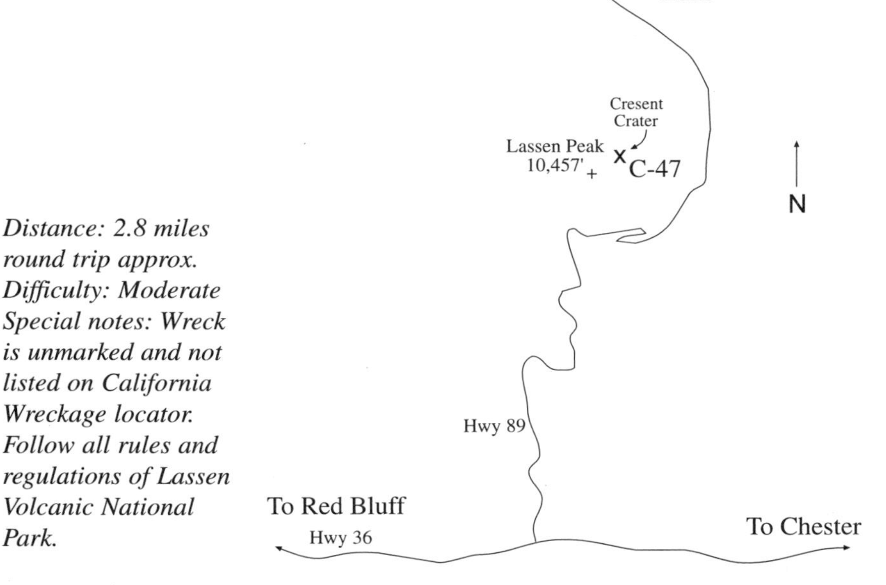

Distance: 2.8 miles round trip approx.
Difficulty: Moderate
Special notes: Wreck is unmarked and not listed on California Wreckage locator. Follow all rules and regulations of Lassen Volcanic National Park.

Date unknown. *Ryan Navion NC-8613* crashed in mountains SW of Glenville in Kern County. Wreck is unmarked.

3/3/53. *Cessna 140 N81041* crashed in bad weather in mountains west of Grass Valley. Wreck is marked. No other data available.

5/24/53. *Beechcraft Bonanza NC-8449A* crashed in storm, killing the pilot and passenger. Wreck is located near Mammoth Lakes, is unmarked and only one wing is visible at the 9,500' level SE of Mammoth Mountain.

5/25/53. *Grumman SA-16A #51-7173 USAF* crashed near Sixty Lake Basin. All five crewmen who parachuted to safety were involved in search for missing Beechcraft. Sierra Club attempted to remove this wreck, but the rugged terrain of Castle Domes holds the bulk of this wreck to this day. Weather was a factor in this accident. Wreckage is marked.

10/18/53. *Stinson 108 NC-8609K* crashed in mountains east of Bass Lake. Pilot survived with serious injuries and was rescued. Weather was a factor in this crash. Site is marked.

4/1/54. A *Piper Cub* crashed while on photo flight over High Sierra. Both persons on board survived crash in Vermilion Basin and were sighted by search plane 4/2/54. Status of wreckage is unknown.

7/24/53. *Cessna 170* crashed, killing two men in night landing near Tunnel Meadows Airstrip. Wreck removed by Sierra Club in 1974.

1/24/55. *Stinson* crashed in mountains near Sierra Community of Colfax less than one mile from Interstate 80. Both occupants of aircraft survived without serious injury. Weather was a factor in this accident. Wreck is removed.

2/14/55. *Globe Swift NC-2378B* crashed in bad weather south of Sierra City near Highway 49, killing the pilot. Wreck is removed.

2/26/55. *Beechcraft Bonanza N576C* crashed in storm south of Mammoth Lakes in high country and exploded. Wreck is unmarked and scattered. Two persons died in crash.

5/31/55. *Aircraft of type unknown* crashed NE of Truckee in Sierra County. Wreck is marked. No other data available.

6/12/55. *Lightplane N2426L* crashed in bad weather northeast of Bullards

Bar Reservoir in Yuba County. No other crash data is available at this time.

9/15/55. *Piper J-3 NC3617A* crashed west of Lake Tahoe in the Desolation Lake Wilderness. Wreck is unmarked and no other data is available.

Date unknown. *Old fabric-covered wreckage* powered by seven cylinder radial engine is located at the 8,000' level of upper Haiwee Canyon SW of Olancha and west of Highway 395.

Date unknown. *Stinson N34642* north of Tehachapi near Emerald Mountain.

Date unknown. *Old aircraft wreck* marked at 39° 00'N and 120° 44'W SE of Forest Hill.

7/29/56. *Lockheed TV-2 US Navy* lies scattered and unmarked in Yosemite National Park SW of Soldier Lake.

8/2/56. *McDonnell F2H-3 US Navy* crashed south of Split Mountain in Taboose Pass. Wreck is scattered and unmarked SW of Big Pine with tail intact.

2/22/57. *Lockheed T-33A #51-14495 USAF* crashed in storm south of Graniteville in Nevada County, killing both crewmen. Wreck is unmarked and scattered at 5,500' level.

5/57. *Lockheed T-33A #52-9232 USAF* crashed following pilot bailout in the Granite Basin region near Lake Helen in Kings Canyon National Park. The pilot survived for eight weeks before being rescued by hikers on July 1, 1957. Air Force investigators did not believe the pilot's story of survival since no wreckage was found. Some wreckage was finally located in 1980s near Mt. Powell, but the pilot had died a few years earlier and did not live to receive his well-deserved official apology. An unofficial search continues in an effort to locate the main impact site of this elusive "T-Bird."

7/28/57. *Cessna N4626C* hit East Spur, killing all on board in cloudy weather. Site is unmarked, west of town of Independence, in Inyo County.

10/57. *Beechcraft Bonanza NC-68104* crashed in bad weather near Hockett Peak NE of Camp Nelson. Wreck is scattered and unmarked. No other data is available.

1/13/58. *North American F-86D California Air National Guard* crashed in bad weather, killing the pilot, 20 miles east of Fresno in Sierra Foothills. Wreck is removed.

9/12/58. *Cessna UC-78 N67355* crashed NE of Emigrant Gap near Spaulding Lake in Nevada County. Wreck is scattered and unmarked. No other data is available.

1/11/59. *Cessna 195 N9839A* crashed SW of Lone Pine near Wonga Peak, killing the pilot. Accident occurred in bad weather and wreck is scattered and unmarked.

1/13/59. *Curtiss C-46F N1240N Slick Airways* hit 9,046' Panther Peak in snow storm, killing both crewmen. Site is in Sequoia National Park east of Giant Forest Village. Major salvage of wreck was undertaken in 1966-67 by someone using a portable smelter. Unmarked debris litters crash site today.

5/2/59. *Piper Commanche N5615P* crashed on west slope of Mammoth Pass at 8,500' level, killing all three persons on board. Site is unmarked near Horseshoe Lake in heavy woods. The author was chased by a large female bear while photographing this wreck in August of 1980. The search for N5615P was not successful until 7/29/59. On 6/11/59 searchers spotted the old Douglas P-70B on Mt. Quarry in Yosemite.

Date unknown. *Vultee BT-13* wreck is located on Mt. Poso north of Bakersfield.

Date unknown. *Howard DGA N67764* is wrecked on Harper Peak east of Bakersfield.

Date unknown. *Luscombe 8A NC3706* is marked on Eagle Peak north of Tehachapi.

6/29/59. *Luscombe 8 N25116* crashed near Bass Lake when pilot flew into blind canyon in clear weather. Pilot died in crash and wreck is removed.

8/8/59. *Globe Swift N3355X* crashed at 6,000' level near Yuba Pass in Sierra County. No other data available.

9/59. *Aircraft, type unknown*, crashed in mountains east of Porterville. No other data available.

1/19/60. *Aercoupe N94858* crashed near Little Whitney Meadow at the 11,000' level, killing three people in an aircraft designed to carry only two persons. Apparently the pilot was attempting to fly his two passengers to the top of Mt. Whitney when they crashed. Wreck was not located until 10/13/60. Weather was not a factor in this accident. Wreck was removed by Sierra Club in 1974.

2/27/60. *Beechcraft T-34 N6186C* crashed in Shasta County, NW of Lake Britton. One man died in this weather-related accident. Status of wreck is not known today.

3/17/60. *Piper Commanche N6047P* hit Patterson Mountain at 8,160' level in bad weather, killing both people on board. Wreck is located on north slope and is unmarked. Site is 40 miles NE of Fresno.

3/26/60. *Stinson N97865* crashed in storm east of Interstate 5 near La Moine in Shasta County. All on board died in crash. Wreck is burned and unmarked.

5/28/60. *Cessna 120 NC-89637* crashed at Hockett Meadows in Sequoia National Park, killing one man and seriously injuring another. Weather was not a factor in this accident. Unwarranted low flying/pilot error was listed as cause. Unmarked wreckage is still visible in trees at edge of meadow.

Stone marker at crash site of P-40 #39-200 USAAF flown by Lt. W.H. Birrell on Grey's Mountain near Bass Lake. (J.K. Lawson) Region 14.

8/18/60. *Grumman TBM NC-109Z* hit 115' tree while fighting forest fire at Independence Lake near Truckee, killing the pilot. Wreck is removed but propeller blade is still visible in tree. Smoke obscured pilot's vision.

10/9/60. *Beechcraft Bonanza* en route from Oakland, California, to Las Vegas, Nevada crashed in cloudy weather on Shadow Mountain. All three persons died in crash. Wreck was not located until 10/17/60. Site is at 4,000' level, in southern Sierra. No other data available.

10/26/60. *Piper Tri-Pacer N2923Z* hit Duncan Peak in Placer County, killing all four persons on board. Weather was bad at time of accident. Status of wreck today is not known.

Date unknown. *Douglas AD-6 #139669 US Navy* crashed in bad weather near Olmstead View near Tuolumne Meadows in Yosemite National Park. Wreck is unmarked and visible. Pilot died in this weather-related accident.

2/25/61. *Beechcraft Bonanza N4499V* crashed in bad weather north of town of Tehachapi in southern Sierra. No other data available.

3/11/61. *Cessna 210 N6588X* crashed in bad weather near town of Quincy in Plumas County. The wreck is scattered and unmarked. No other data is available.

3/16/61. *Cessna 172 N6772X* hit north slope of Mt. Lola in Nevada County in bad weather, killing all on board. Wreck is marked and visible.

6/2/61. *Bell 47G N8474E* crashed west of Highway 395 near community of Sykes in High Sierra. No other information available.

11/9/61. *Cessna 172 N7838X* crashed and burned east of Porterville in foothills. Weather was a factor in this accident that killed two. Wreck is removed.

12/1/61. *North American T-28A* civil registration broke up in flight four miles east of Pine Flat Dam in Fresno County, killing both men on board. Clear air turbulence was listed as a factor in this accident. Wreck is mostly removed.

12/14/61. *Piper Tri-Pacer N8239C* hit Dowd Peak at 4,200' level in bad weather. Four persons died in crash. Site is located 30 miles east of town of San Andreas.

3/9/62. *Ercoupe* crash landed on Owens Mountain west of Highway 395, without injuring the two people on board. Crash site is at 6,000' level and wreck is removed. Pilot error was cited as cause of mishap.

4/27/62. *Piper Tri-Pacer N3416Z* crashed in storm at 8,000' level of Snow Mountain near town of Kingsvale. Three persons died in crash. Wreck is marked, but difficult to see.

5/8/62. *Piper Commanche N7602P* crashed in cloudy weather south of town of Downieville in Sierra County. All on board died in crash. Wreck is unmarked.

5/9/62. *McDonnell F-101B USAF* crashed in bad weather east of Dome Mountain in Siskiyou County. Wreck is scattered and mostly removed.

5/16/62. *Beechcraft Bonanza N477B* crashed in bad weather NE of Red Bluff in foothills. One man died in this crash. Wreck is scattered and marked.

7/62. *Piper Commanche N5069P* crashed at 9,000' level of Stubblefield Canyon, killing all four men on board. Wreckage is located in a remote part of Yosemite National Park, and was not found until 8/7/94 when a hiker stumbled upon debris.

8/16/62. *Stinson 108 N34642* crashed in southern Sierra north of town of Tehachapi. No other data available.

2/18/63. *Cessna 150 N7855E* hit south slope of Mt. Shasta in snowstorm, killing both people on board. Status of wreck is not known.

4/16/63. *Piper Tri-Pacer N5864D* is located SW of town of Bodfish in Kern County. Wreck is intact but unmarked. No other data available.

4/23/63. *Piper Commanche* crash-landed in meadow 15 miles north of Kernville in bad weather. All three people on board escaped with minor injuries. Wreck is removed.

5/16/63. *Piper Colt N8738D* crashed in cloudy weather in trees south of Bucks Lake in Plumas County. No other data available.

8/63 *Northrop P-61B N30020* crashed on fire-fighting flight east of Porterville in foothills. Plane hit trees, killing the pilot.

Douglas C-47A #43-4812

Horizontal stabilizer of a Douglas C-47A #43-4812 near Cresent Crater. See inset map page 161. (G.P. Macha) Region 14.

10/20/63. *Cessna 150 N7869Z* crashed in bad weather west of Truckee north of Highway 80. No other data available.

11/15/63. *Cessna 150 N7243X* crashed in bad weather south of Lake Tahoe near community of Fallen Leaf. No other data available.

12/3/63. *Cessna 150* hit Piute Mountain ten miles south of Lake Isabella, killing both people on board. Accident occurred in snowstorm. Status of wreck is not known.

1/13/64. *Cessna 182 N8867X* crashed two miles west of Huntington Lake at 7,400' level of Mushroom Rock. Accident occurred in snowstorm, killing both people on board. Wreck is removed.

2/20/64. Douglas A-4C #148504 US Navy crashed in bad weather, killing the pilot. Site is located south of June Lake in mountains. Wreck is unmarked and scattered.

2/20/64. *Douglas A-4E #150077 US Navy* crashed in bad weather, killing the pilot. Wreck is scattered and unmarked south of Mammoth Lakes.

3/1/64. *Cessna 172 N72607T* crashed in storm at 6,850' level of Spanish Peak ten miles west of town of Quincy. Pilot died in crash. Wreck is broken up and unmarked.

3/3/64. *Lockheed Constellation N86504 of Paradise Airlines* hit ridge east of Tahoe, killing all eighty-five people on board. Aircraft was en route from San Jose to Reno when it failed to clear ridge by 30'. Faulty altimeter or pilot failure to reset same were listed as potential causes for crash. Wreck is mostly removed, but scattered debris remains at site.

Date unknown. *Beechcraft 35* is reported at 38° 33'N and 120° 25'W with wings removed.

4/5/64. *Cessna 182 N3625U* hit Kenna Ridge on Mt. Lyell at 11,000' level in bad weather. All three persons on board survived with minor injuries and were rescued. Status of wreck today is unknown.

4/5/64. *Beechcraft UC-45J #29581 US Navy* crashed in storm seven miles SW of Mt. Whitney, killing all four men on board. Wreck was highly visible and marked until removed by Sierra Club in 1974.

4/12/64. *Mooney Mk. 20 N870B* crashed in storm at 7,500' level nine miles NE of town of Beckwourth. All three persons on board died in crash. Status of wreck is not known.

4/30/64. *Cessna O-1A NG-121 California Air National Guard* crashed and burned near Highway 50 south of Tahoe.

6/8/64. *Stearman PT-17 N79466* crashed in mountains east of Fresno at 4,500' level. Pilot was seriously injured and wreck is removed. Clouds were a factor in this accident.

6/8/64. *Beechcraft Travelaire N1763G* crashed and burned, killing all three persons on board. Site is near Hume Lake at 4,400' level. Heavy overcast was a factor in this accident. Wreck is unmarked and difficult to see.

6/14/64. *Piper Super Cub N282T* crashed while on Civil Air Patrol search mission, killing both men on board. Wreck is at 9,200' level near North Lake, 20 miles SW of Bishop. Status of wreck today is not known.

6/25/64. *Grumman F7F-3 N7619C* crashed and burned while on fire-fighting mission near Truckee. The pilot died in the crash. Wreck is located near Posser Dam.

7/14/64. *Piper Cherokee N5493W* crashed in mountains west of Reno. Site is in Sierra County. No other data is available.

8/31/64. *Cessna 182 N5507B* reported at 36° 10'N and 119° 23'W at 4,000' level.

11/10/64. *Piper Cherokee N5756W* crashed while on Civil Air Patrol search flight 36 miles NE of Porterville in Sierra Nevada Mountains. Two men died and wreck is burned and unmarked.

12/19/64. *Piper Commanche N5552P* crashed in bad weather, killing both people on board. Wreck is located 13 miles east of Florence Lake in Fresno County. Status of wreckage today is unknown.

2/27/65. *Bell 47G N73998* crashed in High Sierra near Mt. Langley. No other data available.

Date unknown. *Cessna 185 N88450* is unmarked at Groundhog Meadow west of Olancha. May be removed.

3/23/65. *Sikorsky SH-34J #148935 USMC* crashed on Sonora Peak north of Sonora Pass. Wreck is intact but may be removed. No other data available.

5/8/65. *Cessna 172 N8704U* is reported as unmarked at 39° 05'N and 120° 08'W.

5/19/65. *Ryan Navion N91544* crashed in cloudy weather west of Lake Tahoe. All on board perished in this accident. Wreck is unmarked.

6/17/65. *Piper Commanche* crashed in Kings Canyon National Park, near Forester Lake. Both persons on board survived this mishap and were rescued after sustaining only minor injuries. Pilot error was cited as a factor in this accident. Wreck is removed.

7/65. *Waco Biplane N9220* is reported to have crashed west of the town of

Coleville in the Alpine County area. No other data available for this crash.

9/7/65. *Cessna 172 N8282U* crashed south of Tahoe in the Desolation Valley Primitive Area. No other data available.

10/15/65. *Douglas A-4 US Navy* crashed NE of Lindsay in Sierra foothills at 4,000' level. No other data available.

11/11/65. *Cessna 182 N3167A* is unmarked north of Ebbetts Pass.

11/4/65. *Northrop F-5A #63-8376 USAF* crashed 7.5 miles SW of Lone Pine following pilot's successful ejection. Wreck is scattered and unmarked.

11/30/65. *Cessna 182 N8425T* crashed in bad weather in Carson Pass near Highway 88. Wreck is intact in rocky area, but may now be removed. No other data available.

1/16/66. *Grumman S-2A #136542 US Navy* crashed in storm, killing all four men on board. Wreck is visible north of Highway 50 in Desolation Lake Wilderness. Wreckage is burned.

Douglas C-47B #43-49030 USAF crashed in snow storm on 10/26/50 near Independence Lake north of Truckee. Wreck located in the spring of 1951. (R. Koch) Region 14.

2/6/66. An *Aero Commander 500A N9385R* hit fog shrouded Sutter Buttes at the 2,000' level, killing both persons on board. Unmarked parts are still visible at site north of Yuba City in Sutter County.

4/11/66. *Piper Commanche N6423T* crashed in bad weather east of Pinecrest Lake in Tuolumne County, killing all on board. No other data available.

4/12/66. *Cessna 180 N4559B* hit Highland Peak south of Highway 4, killing all on board. Wreck is marked and visible.

5/31/66. *Luscombe 8A N25353* crashed at 7,200' level near town of Little Norway south of Highway 50. Two persons were seriously injured in this pilot-error accident. Wreck is removed.

6/17/66. *Twin-engine lightplane* crashed in bad weather nine miles NW of Mt. Whitney, killing both people on board. Wreck was not located until 6/27/66. Wreck is described as intact, but may have been removed.

Date unknown. *Navion N91691* is reported marked SW of Lake Tahoe at 38° 51'N and 120° 12'W.

Date unknown. *Piper Tri-Pacer* is unmarked at 39° 28'N and 121° 43'W.

7/2/66. *Cessna 172 N8903B* crashed at 10,000' level near Monache Meadows, seriously injuring four persons on board. Pilot error was cited in this clear-weather accident. Wreck was removed by Sierra Club in 1974.

7/10/66. *Douglas A-4B #152789 US Navy* crashed south of Tower Peak in Yosemite National Park. Wreck is scattered, and mostly removed. No other data available.

8/23/66. *Piper Twin Commanche* crashed at 10,000' level near Kearsarge Pass, killing all four people on board. No other data available.

8/30/66. *Cessna 182 N2376R* crashed in the Mokelume Wilderness. Wreck is unmarked and possibly removed. Crash site near Carson Pass.

9/23/66. *Cessna 172* crashed in High Sierra near town of Kirkwood in El Dorado County. No other data available.

10/3/66. *Lightplane* crashed 15 miles south of Tahoe in High Sierra, killing three persons and injuring one. No other data available.

10/6/66. *Piper Cub N7847F* crashed in cloudy weather NW of Mammoth Pool in High Sierra. No other data available.

12/3/66. *Piper Cherokee N6330W* crashed in bad weather near Merced Falls. The pilot survived and was rescued. Wreck is intact and probably removed.

1/29/67. *Beechcraft Bonanza N5132C* crashed in bad weather in Lassen National Park, killing all four persons on board. Status of wreck is mostly removed.

3/29/67. *Cessna 182 N23F* crashed in bad weather north of Breckenridge Mountain, killing the pilot. No other data available.

8/2/67. *LTV A-7 US Navy* collided with a civilian Cessna 210 over Owens Peak NW of China Lake. The pilot of the A-7 and all three people on the Cessna 210 perished. Unmarked wreckage from both aircraft is scattered on Owens Peak.

10/7/67. *Cessna 172 N5915R* flew up a blind canyon near town of Susanville and crashed at 7,500' level. All three people on board escaped with only minor injuries. Intact wreck is removed.

Date unknown. *Cessna 172 N6167E* is wrecked NE of Auburn at 38° 59'N and 121° 01'W.

10/30/67. *Piper Super Cruiser N4557M* crashed in bad weather west of Kennedy Meadow, near community of Dardanelle. One person died and one person was seriously injured. Wreck has been removed.

11/7/67. *Piper Cherokee N5756W* crashed in bad weather at 6,500' level east of town of Springville. Two people died in this accident. Status of wreck is not known.

11/19/67. *Piper Cherokee N9222J* hit mountain west of community of Little Lake, killing two people and seriously injuring two others. Weather was a factor in this crash. The site is located west of Highway 395. Wreck is removed.

12/8/67. *Republic F-105D USAF* crashed in mountains south of Lake Isabella in Kern County. Pilot ejected safely following in-flight malfunction. Wreck is marked near Liebel Peak.

2/10/68. A *Lightplane* hit Pyramid Peak in very bad weather, killing all four persons on board. No other data available.

7/30/68. *Boeing KC-135A USAF* crashed west of Lassen Peak, killing all six men on board. Aircraft exploded and burned following apparent in-flight malfunction. Scattered parts only at crash site.

8/1/68. *Cessna 182* is reported marked at 40° 48'N and 121° 47'W.

8/1/68. *Mooney Mk 20E N528Q NE* of Kyburz, north of Highway 50 is marked.

Date unknown. *Cessna 150 N7343* is south of Lake Tahoe at 38° 52'N and 120° 05'W.

8/17/68. *Beechcraft Bonanza N1235Z* crashed in bad weather at 7,500' level of Squaw Peak in Placer County. Both persons on board died in crash. Status of wreck is unknown.

10/14/68. *Republic F-105D USAF* crashed in mountains 30 miles east of Bakersfield, following in-flight malfunction. Pilot parachuted to safety. Wreck is mostly removed.

11/25/68. *Lightplane* crashed in bad weather 18 miles north of town of Quincy, killing four and seriously injuring one person. No other data is available.

1/11/69. *Piper Cherokee N8407R* crashed on Round Mountain in Shasta County. Two persons died in this weather-related accident. Site is east of Interstate 5 and is mostly removed.

1/17/69. *Cessna 180 N4734B* crashed in bad weather west of Lake Tahoe. Wreck is located near Twin Peaks. No other data available.

1/31/69. *Piper Cherokee N8855W* vanished in snowstorm with four people on board. Wreck was located 5/24/69 near Markleville in Alpine County. Status of wreck is unknown.

2/18/69. *Douglas DC-3 N15570 Mineral County Airlines* disappeared while en route from Hawthorn, Nevada, to Burbank, California. The "Gambler's Special," as this flight was called, carried thirty-five passengers and crew when it vanished in a winter snowstorm. An extensive search was launched on 2/19/69 during the course of which two Civil Air Patrol search planes and an Air Force helicopter crashed. The wreck of the *N15570* was finally located on 8/8/69 by a search aircraft, north of Mt. Whitney at 11,900' level of Hog Back Ridge. Wreck is marked and visible.

2/24/69. *Douglas TA-4F #154654 US Navy* hit ridge north of Mt. Whitney in snowstorm, killing both men on board. Wreck is scattered and unmarked.

2/25/69. A *Douglas A-1E #132435 US Navy* crashed while searching for missing TA-4F, slightly injuring two man crew. Site is located at 12,000' level near Mt. Whitney. Intact wreck is reported removed, but this is not confirmed.

3/16/69. *Beechcraft Bonanza* crashed while engaged in search for "Gambler's Special." One man was seriously injured and two others were hurt in this clear air turbulence accident. Site is near Horton Lake at 11,000' level, 15 miles west of Bishop. Wreck is reported to have been removed.

4/24/69. *Cessna 180 N140F* crashed in storm near Mammoth Pass, killing all four persons on board. Site is at 10,000' level and is removed.

5/69. *Douglas A-3B US Navy* crashed in storm 15 miles SE of Alturas, killing all three men on board.

7/13/69. *Mooney Mk. 20 N3533X* crashed while engaged in search for "Gambler's Special." Both men on board died in crash. Wreck was removed by Sierra Club in 1974 from the 7,600' level west of Big Pine. N3533X had burned on impact.

8/7/69. *Cessna 172* crashed in mountains east of Kernville, with only minor injuries sustained by the four people on board. Wreck was removed.

8/10/69. A *Kaman HH-43B USAF* rescue helicopter crashed 100 yards from the wreck of "Gambler's Special," injuring one man seriously and slightly injuring four others.The helicopter was assisting in recovery operations when accident occurred. Wreck is mostly removed.

11/7/69. *Cessna 172 N4263F* crashed in bad weather at 6,200' level east of Downieville. Both persons on board survived with minor injuries. Wreck is removed.

12/26/69. *Beechcraft Musketeer N3565R* crashed on Bear Mountain near Angels Camp in storm. All three persons on board died in crash. Status of wreck is not known.

12/27/69. *Piper N999E* crashed in storm in Yosemite National Park. No other data available.

Date unknown. *Cessna 177 N29500* is unmarked and scattered north of Alpine.

Date unknown. *Cessna 210 N6721B* is unmarked at 39° 09'N and 120° 17'W.

1/11/70. *Cessna 206 N5085U* crashed in storm near town of Jackson in Amador County. The formal search for this aircraft was canceled after about ten days. However, a privately-organized effort continued, resulting in the dramatic rescue of two persons a full 15 days after the crash. The pilot died on impact, one person suffered serious injury, another escaped with only minor injuries. Site is at 7,500' and is mostly removed.

4/20/70. *Cessna 172* crashed in bad weather east of Fresno in Sierra foothills. Three people died in crash. Wreck is removed.

5/2/70. A *Thorpe T-18* crashed while it was engaged in a Civil Air Patrol search mission, killing both men on board. Site is located near Huntington Lake and wreck is removed.

5/9/70. *Lightplane* crashed in central High Sierra while engaged in search mission for Civil Air Patrol. Two persons died in crash. No other data is available.

5/11/70. *Piper Cherokee N3938T* crashed in storm SW of Lake Tahoe. No other data available.

6/12/70. *Grumman E-1B US Navy* crashed in storm at 10,500' level near Farewell Gap in Sequoia National Forest, killing crew of four men. Wreck is partly removed.

Summer 1970. *Rockwell International OV-10A USMC* crashed on Mt. Lyell at 12,000' level. Both crewmen safely ejected prior to impact and aircraft crash-landed almost intact. Wreck is marked with yellow X's. Pilot error is listed as factor in this accident.

10/17/70. *Lightplane* crashed in eastern High Sierra at the 10,000' level, seriously injuring two persons. Crash site is near town of Olancha.

12/4/70. *LTV A-7 US Navy* crashed in bad weather near Spanish Peak east of Fresno. Pilot died in the crash and scattered wreckage is mostly removed.

12/26/70. *Cessna 177 N2950Q* disappeared with two persons on board while flying in snowstorm near Lake Tahoe. Wreck was not located until 6/71 at 9,600' level of 10,881' mountain peak. Site is located west of Lake Tahoe and wreck is scattered and unmarked.

3/27/71. *Lightplane* crashed and burned in hills near Mariposa Airport. Weather was a factor in this accident that killed three people. No other data available.

5/4/71. *Cessna 182 N3157R* crashed in storm west of Lake Tahoe, killing both persons on board. Status of wreck is not known.

6/28/71. *Piper Cherokee N5125L* crashed in cloudy weather six miles west of Lake Tahoe, killing all four persons on board. Wreck is removed.

7/2/71. *North American T-28B #400558 US Navy* engaged in search mission crashed five miles east of Edison Lake. One man died and one man was seriously injured. Wreck is mostly removed.

This DC-9-31 tail assembly had been dropped some distance from main impact by a helicopter engaged in salvage operations. (R. Urbat) Region 7.

8/28/71. *Douglas TA-4F US Navy* crashed near Mineral King, killing both men on board. Wreck is marked and scattered. Crash occurred during routine training mission.

2/13/72. *Lightplane* crashed in bad weather 25 miles east of town of Sonora in Beardsley Canyon. One person died and one survived with serious injuries. Wreck is removed.

7/4/72. *Lightplane* crashed 25 miles south of Bishop, in Sierra foothills, killing one person and seriously injuring two others. No other data available.

11/17/72. *Piper Super Cub N129T* vanished with one man on board while flying in storm north of town of Tehachapi. Wreck was not located until 4/13/75. Wreck was spotted by Civil Air Patrol searchers who were looking for a missing Cessna 182. N129T had been en route from Carson City, Nevada to Oceanside in San Diego County. Wreck is in Kern County and status unknown.

12/17/72. *Beechcraft Bonanza N4515V* crashed in bad weather north of town of Tehachapi. Wreck is in mountains and may be removed. No other data available.

1/1/73. *Piper PA-28 N92220* west of Little Lake, west of Highway 395.

1/10/73. *Beechcraft N8816A* hit Mt. Wood at 10,000' level while flying in snowstorm, killing all four persons on board. Wreck is located 1.5 miles SW of Parker Lake and is still reported as visible.

1/28/73. *Cessna 182 N21177* crashed in bad weather 15 miles north of Mt. Whitney. All three people survived the crash with minor injuries and were rescued by helicopter. Status of wreck is not known.

2/73. *Lightplane N91792* crashed in bad weather NW of Lake Tahoe, seriously injuring the pilot. Wreck is removed.

4/15/73. *Cessna 150 N60395* north of Tehachapi is unmarked. Pilot died in crash.

4/30/73. *Piper Cherokee N8552N* crashed in bad weather north of Carson Pass. No other data available.

8/2/73. *Grumman TBM* crashed while on fire-fighting mission in Lassen County. Pilot died in crash. Wreck is unmarked and mostly removed.

Date unknown. *Cessna 150 N7173F* crashed near California Hot Springs in Tulare County.

1973. *Piper Cherokee N92220* crashed in mountains near Lake Isabella. No other data available.

10/2/73. *Beechcraft Debonaire* vanished on flight from Mesa, Arizona, to Sacramento, California. Weather was bad over the High Sierra and was a factor in this fatal accident. The wreck was finally discovered on 6/22/74 five miles NE of Florence Lake. Three people had perished in this crash. Wreck is mostly removed.

10/25/73. *Lightplane* crashed in bad weather near community of Oakhurst in Madera County. One man died and one survived with serious injuries. Wreck is removed.

3/11/74. *Lightplane* hit tall trees on mountain ridge in bad weather, killing all three people on board. Crash site is near Columbia State Park. Wreck is removed.

4/25/74. *Cessna 150 N7173F* crashed in mountains NE of Porterville, killing both people on board. Weather was a factor in this accident. Status of wreck is unknown.

6/8/74. *Champion N11094* crashed in mountains west of Highway 395 in Alpine county. No other data available.

6/9/74. *Lightplane* crashed in bad weather in upper Dry Creek Canyon, NW of Mammoth Lakes, killing all four persons on board. Crash site is in Mono County. Status of wreck is not known.

9/23/74. *Mooney Mk. 21 N6727U* at 10,000' level 38° 36'N and 119° 51W.

12/16/74. *Lightplane* crashed in bad weather NW of Lake Tahoe. No other data available.

12/23/74. *Cessna 414 N41412* crashed while flying in severe winter storm, killing all eight persons on board. Wreck is upside down and visible near Wilson Lake in Plumas County.

1/2/75. *Beechcraft Duke* stalled and crashed in clear weather, killing all five people on board. Wreck is removed from site five miles from Mammoth Lakes Airport.

1/5/75. *Helio Currier* crashed in bad weather west of lake Tahoe. Site is in Placer County. No other data available.

2/8/75. A *Cessna 182 N52678* hit Post Peak in bad weather, killing both persons on board. Wreck is at 10,700' level and is marked.

4/9/75. *Cessna 182 N3761A* crashed in bad weather in mountains NE of Bakersfield. All four persons on board died in this accident. Status of wreck is not known.

4/26/75. A *Cessna 182 N5958B* hit Mt. Rose in bad weather, killing both people on board. Site is unmarked west of Lake Tahoe.

6/28/75. *Piper N5703Y* crashed in mountains east of Porterville. No other data available.

10/6/75. *Piper Seneca* crashed in bad weather SW of Carson Pass. No other data available.

10/10/75. *Cessna 310 N818V* hit ridge south of Mt. Darwin, killing all on board. Wreck is unmarked and scattered.

4/10/76. *Bellanca N86927* crashed in High Sierra east of Fresno near Pine Flat, killing the pilot. Weather was a factor in this accident. No other data available.

4/26/76. *Cessna 182 N52855* en route from Oakland in the San Francisco Bay area to Furnace Creek in Death Valley National Monument crashed in Shepard's Pass at 11,800' level. All three persons on board survived the impact but two, including the pilot, died subsequently. The lone survivor, Ms. Lauren Elder, hiked more than twenty miles to finally reach help in the town of Independence on Highway 395. Ms. Elder's epic story of survival is available in her book, *I Alone Survived.* Status of wreck is marked but may now be removed. High winds sometimes referred to as the "Sierra Wave" were a factor in this accident. The crash site was only 15' below the crest.

5/25/76. *Beechcraft T-42 US Army* crashed in High Sierra 18 miles SW of Bishop, killing all three men on board. The wreck is located in very rugged terrain. No other data available.

6/18/76. *Beechcraft Musketeer* crashed in cloudy weather near town of Susansville in Lassen County. Two people died in this accident. Status of wreck is not known.

7/30/76. *Cessna 182 N4652K* hit 11,000' ridge at eastern boundary of Kings Canyon National Park, killing all four persons on board. Status of wreck is not known.

10/2/76. *Lockheed Loadstar N80BD* disappeared in bad weather on a flight reputed to have involved the transportation of illegal substances. Wreck was discovered in frozen lake in Yosemite National Park. The two-man crew died in the crash of this Howard 500 conversion.

10/10/76. *Cessna 150* crashed in box canyon near community of Kernville, killing the pilot. Weather was clear at time of crash. Pilot flew into canyon and could not clear rim. Wreck is removed.

Date unknown. *McDonnell F-4D #65-0766 USAF* near Bald Mountain NW of Little Lake on Highway 395.

Date unknown. *Cessna 172 N5295R* is unmarked at 39° 31'N and 120° 40'W.

Date unknown. *Beechcraft 35 N9442Y* is wrecked in Greenhorn Mountains NE of Bakersfield.

5/21/77. *American Yankee* crashed in cloudy weather 20 miles west of Lake Tahoe. Both persons on board survived the accident with injuries. Wreck is removed.

5/22/77. *Lightplane* crashed in cloudy weather on Interstate 80 in Donner Pass. All four persons on board survived the crash landing without injury. Aircraft removed.

7/2/77. *Helicopter* crashed near Monache Meadows while on fire-fighting mission. No one was injured and helicopter was removed. Site was in Golden Trout Wilderness.

7/3/77. *Helicopter* operated by National Park Service crashed near Mt. Darwin in Kings Canyon National Park. Two of the three men on board were seriously injured. The accident occurred in high-wind conditions as helicopter attempted to remove body of mountain climber from Mt. Darwin.

8/26/77. *Cessna 182* crashed on Highway 50 in High Sierra following mid-air collision. All four persons on board were killed. Wreck was immediately removed. The other aircraft involved made a safe landing.

8/28/77. *Cessna 177 N30748* crashed in mountains south of Lake Tahoe in El Dorado County. Two persons died and two persons were seriously injured. The emergency locator transmitter on board the aircraft was responsible for a timely rescue that saved two lives. Status of wreck is unknown.

9/17/77. *Cessna 177 N30748* crashed into 7,000' Needle Peak west of Lake Tahoe in Placer County. Two persons died in this weather-related accident. Aircraft had been en route from San Diego to Reno when crash occurred.

10/2/77. *Piper Tri-Pace*r crashed at 11,000' level in King's Canyon National Park with serious injuries for one person and minor injuries for another. Pilot error and downdrafts were a factor in this accident.

11/27/77. *Piper PA-28 N3972R* crashed in bad weather in a remote area of King's Canyon National Park, killing all four men on board. Status of wreck is not known. Site is near Kearsarge Pass.

2/10/78. *Cessna 210* crashed in bad weather near Mammoth Lakes Airport at 7,200' level. All five people on board perished. Wreck is removed.

2/19/78. *Cessna 170 N46266* crashed in bad weather on 12,500' peak in King's Canyon National Park. Both people on board survived and were eventually rescued by helicopter. Heavy snow cushioned the impact and only minor injuries resulted for the pilot and his passenger. Status of wreck not known. Site is near Kearsarge Pass.

Date unknown. *Piper PA-28 N4180P* reported at 38° 56'W and 120° 24'W.

Date unknown. *Beechcraft 35 N3704N* is marked at 39° 24'N and 120° 37'W.

Date unknown. *Mooney Mk. 21 N8110E* SW of Mammoth Lakes near Lion Peak is unmarked.

2/78. *Beechcraft Twin* crashed in bad weather eight miles north of Mammoth Lakes Airport, seriously injuring the pilot. Wreck is removed.

3/4/78. *Cessna 411* crashed, hitting Haskell Peak in bad weather and killing all four persons on board. Site is in Sierra County north of Lake Tahoe and west of highway 395.

4/29/78. *Lightplane* crashed while flying in poor weather in Kearsarge Pass at the eastern border of King's Canyon National Park. One person died and one survived with serious injuries. Wreck is mostly removed. No other data.

5/14/78. *Cessna 182 N7358R* crashed in cloudy weather 30 miles west of Truckee, killing all three people on board. Status of wreck is not known.

7/5/78. *Piper Seneca* crashed in cloudy weather near Badger Pass ski resort, killing all five persons on board. Aircraft exploded and burned on impact. Wreck is removed.

11/12/78. *Grumman Lynx* hit Piute Mountain at 7,200' level in bad weather, killing both persons on board. Site is in Kern County south of town of Kernville. Wreck is removed.

2/21/79. A *Lightplane* hit Paper Cabin Ridge in bad weather, killing both people on board. Site is five miles SE of Tuolumne in Tuolumne County. Wreck was located on 2/25/79 and is now removed.

8/21/79. *Lightplane* crashed 30 miles SW of Mammoth Lakes while flying in thunder storm. Both persons on board perished. Status of wreck is not known.

Patric J. Macha and a landing gear leg from Lockheed P-38L USAAF that crashed below Mt. Wilson on 9/20/44 killing the pilot. (C. Killians) Region 14.

11/4/79. *Lightplane* crashed near Mammoth Lakes in bad weather, killing the pilot. No other data available.

11/22/79. *Cessna 172* hit Mt. Lassen in bad weather, killing all three people on board. Wreck is visible and unmarked.

11/24/79. *Piper Commanche* hit Eagle Peak in Modoc County near town of Alturas, killing all three persons on board. Status of wreck today is not known.

2/16/80. *Lightplane* crashed west of community of Inyokern in the High Sierra, killing both persons on board. Weather was a factor in this accident. No other data available.

3/2/80. *Douglas A-26/Smith-Tempo Conversion N4220A* crashed in bad weather six miles east of Georgetown in El Dorado County. All four men on board were killed. Aircraft was on a weather research mission for the Nevada Institute when accident occurred. Status of wreck is unknown.

Date unknown. *Piper Arrow N3672B* SW of Lake Almanor is unmarked.

3/3/80. *Piper Cherokee 6* crashed in storm one mile south of Lake Tahoe Airport in El Dorado County. All five persons on board were killed. Wreck is removed.

Date unknown. *Piper PA-28* crashed SE of South Lake Tahoe Freel Peak. Wreck is unmarked.

Date unknown. *Cessna 150 N7869Z* lies wrecked and unmarked at 39° 22'N and 120° 20'W.

5/25/80. *Cessna 172* crashed in bad weather near Tinkers Gap while on a flight from Lake Tahoe. Both persons on board survived the crash, but died of injuries and exposure before rescuers located crash site on 5/28/80. Wreck is removed.

2/14/81. *Piper PA-28 N9431W* is reported unmarked at 39° 16'N and 120°18'W.

3/19/81. *Cessna 210* crashed in bad weather near Francis Lake, NW of Bishop, killing both people on board. Wreck is scattered and unmarked.

4/9/81. *Cessna 150 N4611P* is unmarked at 39° 36'N and 121° 46'W.

Date unknown. *Cessna 172 N7840G* crashed SE of Mineral King near Rainbow Mountain.

Date unknown. *Mooney Mk. 20 N1942Y* is reported wrecked SE of Mono Lake near Sagehen Peak.

8/3/81. *Piper PA-28 N2300T* is located NE of Luther Pass. Wreck is unmarked.

Date unknown. *Cessna 150 N74020* crashed SW of Lee Vining near Mt. Dana.

1/3/82. *Grumman Tiger N28912* crashed in stormy weather in Tioga Pass, killing two persons and injuring one. The sole survivor, an eleven-year-old boy, stayed alive for five days huddled inside the wreckage. He suffered severe frostbite on his feet and legs. The crash site is located at the 11,100' level of the Sierra Nevada in Yosemite National Park. Wreck is removed.

2/14/82. *Helicopter* engaged in logging operations crashed near community of Sloat in Plumas County. One man died and another was seriously injured. Wreck is removed.

2/22/82. *Piper PA-28 N3646R* is reported at 39° 03'N and 120° 21'W. Wreck is unmarked.

5/82. *LTV A-7E US Navy* crashed in High Sierra near Lone Pine, killing the pilot. Wreck is scattered and partly removed. No other data available.

5/10/82. *Lightplane* hit NE slope of Mt. Shasta in bad weather, killing all four persons on board. Status of wreck is not known.

5/12/82. *Cessna 172 N2996E* crashed near El Portal. Wreck is unmarked.

6/20/82. *Cessna 337 N1378L* crashed west of Inyokern and north of Walker Pass. Wreck is unmarked.

6/23/82. *Helicopter* on rescue mission to assist car accident victims crashed and killed all three people on board. Accident site was at Brightman's Flat at 6,200' level in Tuolumne County. Wreck is removed.

9/17/82. *Cessna 182 N42488* crashed while flying in Feather River Canyon, killing all four persons on board. Crash site is in Plumas County and wreck is removed. No other data available.

9/30/82. *Mooney Mk. 20 N40224H* crashed near Tom's Place close to Highway 395. Wreck is unmarked.

12/7/82. *Piper PA-28 N5468T* is listed as unmarked at 39° 05'N and 120° 16'W.

1983. *Lightplane* crashed in Desolation Wilderness, killing one person and slightly injuring another. Accident site is in El Dorado County. Status of wreck not known.

1/12/83. *Hughes 500D N10948* crashed on Bloody Mountain SE of Mammoth Lakes. Status of wreck is unknown.

2/28/83. *Beechcraft Baron N17993* crashed in bad weather NE of Sonora Pass. Two people onboard died. Wreck is partly removed and is unmarked.

5/23/83. *Varieze N882BF* is located at 39° 40'N and 120° 35'W. Status of wreck is unknown.

7/31/83. *Bell UH-1N US Navy* crashed at 9,500' level near Hortense Lake. Six men were seriously injured and one man sustained minor injuries. Accident occurred while on search mission for missing hikers. Site is about 70 miles NE of Fresno. Wreck is removed.

8/13/83. *Ercoupe-415C N94369* crashed near Alta Sierra while en route from Bakersfield to Kernville. Engine failure was listed as the cause of this accident that killed the pilot. Wreck was located 8/15/83. Status of wreck is unknown.

8/15/83. *Lightplane* engaged in search mission for missing Ercoupe crashed six miles north of Kernville, killing two men and seriously injuring another. Wreck is mostly removed.

8/22/83. *Helicopter* crashed while engaged in logging operations eight miles north of Shaver Lake in Fresno County. Two men died in this accident. Wreck is removed.

1983. *Lightplane* crashed on NE slope of Bear Mountain in bad weather, killing the pilot. Site is north of the town of Keene in Kern County. Wreck is removed.

Date unknown. *Sailplane N3833A* reported crashed SE of Pine Flat near Dalton Mountain. No other data is available for this crash.

Date unknown. *Grumman Cheetah N9945U* is located at 39° 47'N and 121° 44'W. Wreck is unmarked.

12/1/83. *Cessna 172 N6134E* is reported unmarked at 39° 21'N and 120° 22'W.

Date unknown. *Bell Jet Ranger N7491S* crashed NW of Big Pine in the Inyo National Forest near Sugarloaf Mountain.

5/19/84. *Cessna 150 N63557* crashed on Piute Peak about ten miles south of Lake Isabella in Kern County. Two persons on board survived with minor injuries. Wreck is removed. The pilot error was listed as the cause of this accident.

6/1/84. *Piper PA-28 N56981* is wrecked NW of Olancha near Ash Meadow. No other data available.

8/28/84. *Piper PA-28* lies wrecked east of Bakersfield near Caliente in foothills. Wreck may be removed.

11/21/84. *Piper Seneca N2245* is reported at 36° 49'N and 118° 20'W.

Chris Killian and son excavating wreck of Lockheed PV-1 on Sierra Pelona Ridge. (P. J. Macha) Region 7.

Date unknown. *Cessna 172 N7372S* crashed east of community of Woodlake near Hockett Lakes. No other data available.

2/85. *Lightplane* crashed in mountains west of community of China Lake, killing two persons. Weather was a factor in this accident. Wreck is in Kern County and is mostly removed.

1985. *Helicopter* crashed at 8,800' level near Monache Meadows, seriously injuring three people on board. Site is in Tulare County and is removed. No other data available.

11/12/85. *Lightplane* crashed in bad weather 20 miles NE of town of Auburn in Placer County. Three people died in this accident. The wreck is mostly removed.

12/8/85. *Lightplane* hit Pyramid Peak in the Desolation Wilderness of El Dorado County, killing all three people on board. Weather was a factor in this accident. Status of wreck is not known.

3/15/86. *Beechcraft Bonanza* crashed in bad weather nine miles south of Lake Tahoe, killing all three people on board. Wreck is unmarked.

Beechcraft Bonanza N2PA crashed in bad weather near 11,513' Tioga Peak killing the pilot. Accident occurred in February of 1996. (Roger Nichols) Region 14.

6/30/86. *Grumman S-2* crashed while on fire-fighting mission near Angels Camp in Calaveras County. Two men on board perished in this accident. Wreck is burned and partly removed. Aircraft was operated by California Division of Forestry.

11/17/86. *Cessna 150* crashed in cloudy weather near the summit of Lookout Peak at the 8,200' level. Both men on board were killed. Site is near Lake Isabella in Kern County. Wreck is removed.

3/18/87. *Lightplane* crashed in cloudy weather, killing all four persons on board. Site is located two miles south of Jamestown in Tuolumne County. Wreck is removed.

5/20/87. *McDonnell Douglas TF-18 US Navy* disappeared over the eastern Sierra Nevada while on a training flight. An extensive search failed to find any trace of the missing plane until 6/20/88 when a ground search party located the scattered wreckage in the Hoover Wilderness. The TF-18 had impacted on a near vertical cliff and exploded. Both crewmen died instantly in this accident. Wreck is scattered and unmarked in Mono County.

6/10/87. *Cessna 172 N55186* crashed near University Peak which is NW of Lone Pine in Death Valley. No other is data available for this accident.

7/17/87. *North American T-28* listed SE of Mammoth Pool Reservoir. Yellow X's painted on rocks at crash site near Westfall Creek.

Date unknown. *Cessna 152 N24505* is reported at 39° 07'N and 120° 28'W.

7/28/87. *Beechcraft T-34B US Navy Reserve* crashed in cloudy weather 80 miles north of Reno in the High Sierra, killing both men on board. Status of this wreck is not known.

7/28/87. *Lightplane* crashed in cloudy weather at 10,400' level near Tioga Pass. Two persons died and four others were seriously injured. Wreck is mostly removed.

7/87. *Globe Swift N77792* crashed and burned in the Sierra Nevada Mountains 30 miles NE of Porterville in Tulare County. One man died and another man was seriously injured. Clear air turbulence was listed as a factor in this accident. Crash site is near Mountain Home Conservation Camp and wreck is removed.

5/29/88. *Cessna 421 N98683* disappeared on a flight from Rialto in southern California to the Lake Tahoe area in north-central California. There were four persons on board the aircraft. The wreckage was located on 6/5/88 by a Civil Air Patrol plane about 18 miles SW of Mammoth Lakes in the central High Sierra. Site of this weather-related fatal accident is in Madera County. Wreck is marked and visible.

7/31/88. *Cessna 177* crashed in upper end of Vidette Meadow in Kings Canyon National Park, killing three men and seriously injuring one man. The aircraft had been en route from Oakland, California, to Las Vegas, Nevada. Crash site is at the 10,000' level and wreck is to be removed. Pilot error is listed as a factor in this accident.

8/12/88. *Beechcraft Baron of the US Forest Service* crashed while leading fire-fighting aircraft attacking a wildfire in the Sequoia National Forest NE of Bakersfield. The pilot was killed in the crash. Mechanical failure may have been a cause of this accident. Wreck is burned and partly removed.

8/23/88. *Lightplane* crashed on 3,300' Mt. Bullion in Mariposa County, killing the pilot. Engine malfunction may have been a cause of this accident. Crash site is near Yosemite-Mariposa Airport and wreck is removed.

11/12/88. *Beechcraft Bonanza N5594D* is listed as unmarked at 39° 05'N and 122° 10'W.

8/6/89. *Piper Cherokee N6274W* crashed in the Pioneer Lakes Basin region north of Edison Lake. Both men on board were killed in this pilot error accident. Wreckage was located by hikers on 8/12/89. Wreck is burned and unmarked. Site is in Fresno County.

10/28/89. *Cessna 177 N30228* is reported at 38° 52'N and 120° 11'W. Wreck is unmarked.

11/89. *Cessna 182 N52678* disappeared over the High Sierra east of Giant Grove in Sequoia National Park. Wreck was discovered SE of Barton Peak by hikers 8/90. No other data available.

1/13/90. *Cessna 172 N7581U* crashed NW of Lone Pine near 13,630' Table Mountain.

1/14/90. *Lightplane* crashed in snowstorm near Tom's Place west of Highway 395. All three persons on board were killed when their aircraft impacted a cloud-enshrouded mountain. Status of wreckage is not known.

5/20/90. *Luscombe Sedan N71653* crashed, killing four persons while on a night flight from central California to Los Angeles. The crash site is located 14 miles east of Placerville in El Dorado County. One wing is still visible hanging in a tree. Wreck is not marked and may be removed.

9/20/90. *Two Boeing Vertol CH-46 US Navy helicopters* made forced landings while flying in formation near Lobdell Lake in the Sweetwater Mountains, after encountering severe turbulence. None of the nine men aboard the two aircraft were seriously injured, and both aircraft have been removed. Site was near Bridgeport in Mono County.

5/3/91. *Mooney Mk. 21 N9624M* is reported wrecked at 39° 48'N and 120° 59'W.

1/5/92. *Cessna 421* crashed in snowstorm south of Mammoth Lakes and east of Highway 395 atop 11,472' Red Mountain. Four persons died and two survived this weather-related accident. Wreck is reported mostly removed.

10/1/92. A *Douglas DC-7B N848D* crashed and exploded while on a fire-fighting mission in the El Dorado National Forest. Both crewmen were killed and wreckage is scattered and unmarked.

1970. Two Marine Corps officers ejected safely from a Rockwell International OV-10A "Bronco" before it crashed on Mt. Lyell at 12,000' level. The Park service blew up the virtually intact plane to make it less visible. (G.P. Macha) Region 14.

11/12/93. *Beechcraft Bonanza* crashed between Edison and Florence Lakes in the John Muir Wilderness at the 10,000' level, killing all four persons on board. The plane was en route from San Jose to Death Valley at the time of related crash.

2/13/94. *Piper PA-28* crashed near South Lake Tahoe, killing the pilot. The smashed, unmarked wreck is located in heavily-wooded Tucker Flat area of El Dorado County. Weather was a factor in this accident.

11/27/94. *Maule M-5 Rocket* crashed at the 8,000' level on the south slope of Kern Peak in Inyo County. The pilot and both of his passengers survived the crash. However, the ELT was inoperable and temperatures were very low at night, contributing to the deaths of the injured passengers. The pilot hiked for nine days before reaching the town of Olancha on Highway 395.

3/23/95. *Beechcraft Debonaire* crashed in storm on Wheeler Ridge at the 9,200' level on east slope of the High Sierra. Wreck was located on 3/30/95 with the body of the pilot still aboard.

7/95. *Bell 206* hit power lines in the Sequoia National Forest, killing both persons on board. Wreck is burned and unmarked in Tulare County.

12/8/96. *Beechcraft BE-35* with one man on board was listed as missing in storm 15 miles west of Squaw Valley. Wreckage is not expected to be located until spring of 1997.

2/96. *Beechcraft Bonanza N2PA* crashed in bad weather west of Lee Vining near Tioga Peak killing the pilot. Wreck is unmarked and visible as of 7/96.

Region 15

The North Coast Ranges of California comprise the majority of Region 15. The boundaries of this area include the Pacific Ocean on the west, the Oregon border on the north, Interstate 5 on the east, San Pablo Bay, and the Golden Gate on the south. This area contains dense forests of redwood, pine, and fir trees. The highest peak is 9,038' Mt. Eddy. Here also are the Trinity Alps, Salmon, Klamath, and Siskiyou Mountains. Locating wreck sites in this area can be very difficult because of the thick undergrowth, towering trees, and difficult weather conditions. More than ninety aircraft have crashed within the limits of this region.

11/2/41. *Two Curtiss P-40s USAAF* hit Bald Peak in Marin County near Hamilton Field, killing both pilots. Weather was a factor in these crashes that marked the last fatal losses in a disastrous two weeks for 57th Pursuit Squadron pilots flying nineteen P-40s from March Field in Riverside County to McClellan Field near Sacramento. Altogether, eight aircraft were destroyed and four pilots killed. Five of the aircraft went down in the High Sierra, two in Region 15, and one bailout south of San Francisco in Region 13. Only small amounts of wreckage remain visible at the Bald Peak sites today.

1942. *Consolidated B-24D #41-24262 USAAF* crashed in bad weather NE of Seaview in Sonoma County. Site is unmarked.

Date unknown. *Grumman F4F US Navy* is reported at 41° 08'N and 122° 52'W. Site is unmarked.

Date unknown. *Bell P-39N #42-9120 USAAF* crashed at 1,500' level on Rancher Hill SW of Down Hill. Wreck is scattered and unmarked. Reported position is 39° 02'N and 122° 22'W.

2/3/42. *Martin B-26A USAAF* crashed in bad weather, killing all on board. Wreck was not immediately located. Site was in Trinity Alps NW of Trinity Center. All wreckage was removed by Sierra Club as clean-up project in mid 1970s.

1/21/43. *Martin Philippine Clipper NC-14715* crashed in Coast Ranges south of Ukiah in Mendocino County. Aircraft was en route from Hawaiian

Islands to San Francisco when it crashed in bad weather, killing all nineteen people on board. Although unmarked, a considerable amount of wreckage remains at site in ravine near VOR station. A monument now marks this historically-important wreck.

5/30/43. *Boeing B-17F USAAF* crashed in bad weather on Leech Lake Mountain, killing all on board. Wreck is marked and is situated in NE Mendocino County at 6,300' level.

Date unknown. *Military wreckage* is reported east of Lake Berryessa, dating from 1942-43. Olive drab parts are visible just west of Yolo County line.

6/16/44. *Lockheed P-38J-20 #44-23412 USAAF* crashed one mile north of town of Occidental. Only small unmarked parts remain in area of heavy undergrowth.

11/29/44. *Martin PBM-3 US Navy* hit Mt. Tamalpais in bad weather, killing all eight crewmen. While some wreckage is removed, much unmarked metal remains at site just north of San Francisco. Wreck is on east slope of mountain.

Boeing B-17F USAAF flap section on Leech Lake Mountain. Crash date 5/30/43. (Jim Rowan) Region 15.

Date unknown. *Lockheed P-38 USAAF* hit mountain near Lake Sonoma. The pilot was killed while attempting to bail-out. Status of wreck is not known.

1945. *Lockheed P-38J USAAF* crashed east of Annapolis in NW Sonoma County. Wreck is scattered, unmarked and partly removed at 600' level.

1945. *Vought F4U US Navy* crashed on Mt. Tamalpais following a mid-air collision. Pilot bailed out and his plane crashed in heavy undergrowth on west slope of mountain. Unmarked parts remain at site.

11/14/45. *Grumman F6F-3 #25980 US Navy* crashed in bad weather SW of Dunsmuir. Wreck is covered and unmarked. Pilot died in crash.

12/3/45. *Vultee BT-13A #41-9669 USAAF* hit St. John's Mountain SW of Orland. Wreck is marked and visible.

6/6/47. *Grumman TBM-3 #86096* crashed north of Snowden in Scotts Mountains. No other data available.

6/6/47. *Piper Cub NC-3620M* crashed in mountains west of Clear Lake. Wreck is marked but hard to see. No other data available.

1949. A *Grumman F6F-5 #94455 US Navy Reserve* vanished on routine training flight from Moffet Field. Wreck was not found until 1971 near Clear Lake in dense forest. Remains of pilot were removed and wreck was marked.

Date unknown. *North American F-82F USAF* crashed in mountains NE of Willits. Wreck is marked and visible. No other data available.

12/22/48. *Aircraft type unknown* reported at 40° 49'N and 122° 07'W. Wreckage is unmarked.

Date unknown. *Military aircraft type unknown* at 41° 08'N and 122° 52'W. Wreck is scattered, unmarked and thought to be WW II vintage.

Date unknown. *Beechcraft JRB-4 #86096 US Navy* is wrecked and visible at 41° 11'N and 122° 58'W.

Date unknown. *Beechcraft C-45 USAF* crashed in mountains west of Novato. Wreck is unmarked and few parts remain.

2/23/51. *Grumman F6F US Navy Reserve* crashed in bad weather near Vacaville in Solano County, killing the pilot. Status of wreck today is not known.

7/1/52. *Stinson Voyager NC-9412K* is marked and visible at 40° 43'N and 122° 21'W.

11/1/53. *Cessna 195 NC-1099D* crashed in bad weather near Minersville, killing the pilot. Wreck is marked and visible.

8/25/54. *North American TB-25J USAF* hit mountain ridge 500' below top, killing all eight men on board. Only small parts remain NE of Santa Rosa. Weather was a factor in this crash.

8/26/54. Two *North American F-86F USAF fighters* collided and crashed north of Lake Berryessa in Napa County. Wrecks are marked and parts are still visible from the air.

8/26/54. *North American TB-25J USAF* crashed at the 2,000' level NW of Winters in Portugee Canyon. Eight servicemen died on this night training mission from Mather AFB. Site is unmarked with small parts visible in Napa County.

8/26/54. Two *Douglas AD-6s #135245 and #135264* hit Mt. St. Helen in Sonoma County, killing both pilots. Wrecks are marked and tails are still visible. Both aircraft were assigned to Attack Squadron VA-195. Weather was once again a factor in this accident.

8/25/55. A *McDonnell F2H-2 #123344 US Navy* plane crashed following a malfunction NE of Santa Rosa in Sonoma County. Wreck is scattered and unmarked.

2/19/56. *Lockheed T-33A #51-9307 USAF* crashed in bad weather north of Calistoga on Mt. St. Helena in Napa County. Wreck is scattered, unmarked, and mostly removed.

9/16/56. *Stinson N3300P* crashed on south slope of Snow Mountain at 3,500' level in cloudy weather. Wreck site is in Colusa County and is unmarked.

3/10/57. *Piper Super Cub N1146A* crashed during a storm in rugged timber country east of Ukiah at 2,000' level. Wreck is unmarked in Mendocino County.

2/13/58. *Douglas AD-4N #135048* crashed following bail-out by two crewmen in Mendocino County, east of Point Arena at 1,500' level and south of Highway 253. Wreck is marked.

3/10/58. *Piper Cub NC-3695M* crashed NW of Vacaville in Napa County at 2,000' level. Wreck was marked but is no longer visible.

8/9/58. *Stinson N8860K* crashed south of Cecilville in Trinity Alps of Siskiyou County. Wreck is marked and visible.

5/1/60. *Piper N25264P* crashed in bad weather SW of Red Bluff in Tehama County. Wreck is unmarked.

7/16/60. *Cessna 172 N4661* crashed in cloudy weather SE of Point Arena. Wreck is marked.

4/30/61. *Cessna 172* hit ridge west of Mill Valley in bad weather, killing all three people on board. Wreck is removed.

11/19/61. *Piper Commanche N5884P* crashed in hills SE of Santa Rosa. Wreck is scattered and unmarked near Glen Ellen.

1/12/62. *Piper Tri-Pacer N3248Z* crashed and burned in bad weather NE of Healdsburg. Wreck is unmarked at 1,000' level and may be removed.

3/9/62. *Piper Tri-Pacer N44324* crashed north of St. John Mountain in Glenn County. Wreck is unmarked.

4/62. *Piper Tri-Pacer* hit south of Yolla Bolly Mountain in Tehama County. Status of wreck today is not known.

5/18/62. *Beechcraft 95 N506K* crashed north of Trinity Center in Trinity County. Status of wreck is not known.

8/4/62. *Beechcraft 35 N3050V* struck Laughlin Ridge in Mendocino County, killing all four persons on board. Wreck is scattered and unmarked.

9/7/62. *Piper Commanche N5861P* crashed in mountains east of Eureka. Weather was cloudy at time of accident. No other data available.

9/24/62. *Grumman F7F-3 N7625C* crashed while on fire-fighting mission near the town of Callahan in Siskiyou County. The pilot was killed and wreckage is scattered and unmarked.

10/8/62. *Piper Apache N3125P* crashed in bad weather 40 miles SE of Eureka, killing all three people on board. Wreck is unmarked and overgrown in Coast Ranges.

5/6/63. *Cessna 310 N3024R* crashed and burned in cloudy weather north of Shelter Cove in Humbolt County. All on board perished in this accident. Wreck is unmarked, but some parts are visible.

7/6/63. *Erocoupe N94481* crashed south of town of Scotia in Humbolt County. Wreck is marked, intact, and visible.

8/22/64. *Mooney Mk. 20 N5241B* hit ridge at 2,400' level north of St. Helena. One person was killed and two were seriously injured in a clear-weather, pilot-error accident.

11/27/64. *Piper Tri-Pacer N8696C* crashed in bad weather in hills NW of Guinda, killing the pilot. Wreck is removed.

12/12/64. *Cessna 310 N3016D* crashed in storm at 2,100' level near Napa, killing the pilot. Wreck is removed.

12/19/64. *Cessna 175 N7226M* crashed in hills at 1,000' level near Cloverdale in Sonoma County. Pilot was killed in this weather-related accident. Wreck is removed.

Date unknown. *Piper Cub N55930* is listed as marked at 39° 23'N and 122° 48'W.

Date unknown. *Cessna 170 N6621C* is reported as unmarked at 39° 07'N and 122° 42'W.

Date unknown. *Cessna 120 N2705N* is listed as marked at 39° 34'N and 123° 00'W.

7/2/65. *Emigh Trojan N8321H* crash-landed NW of Vacaville with minor injuries to pilot. Wreck is intact and is removed.

11/14/65. *Piper PA-22 N7345D* is listed as wrecked east of Inverness in Marin County. Wreck is unmarked.

2/22/66 *Piper Commanche N5337P* crashed north of Lake Pillsbury in bad weather, killing everyone on board. Status of wreck today is not known.

2/23/66. *Lightplane* crashed in storm, killing all three people on board. Crash site is in wilderness area of Humbolt County.

4/10/66. *Piper Tri-Pacer N8014D* crashed in cloudy weather near Point Arena. No other data available.

8/19/66. *Douglas A-4C US Navy* crashed in mountains west of Garberville in Humbolt County. Wreck is scattered and unmarked.

Date unknown. *Cessna 172* crashed at 1,500' level near Shelter Cove. One person was killed and three were seriously injured. Accident occurred in poor weather. Status of wreck not known.

3/11/67. *Cessna 195 N9388A* crashed on Shoemaker Bally Mountain in the

Ryan PT-22 #41-5748

Patric J. Macha, my son, in November 1976 at Ryan PT-22 #41-5748 crash site in the San Jacinto Mtns. at age eight. (G.P. Macha) Region 4.

Trinity Mountains during a winter storm. The aircraft with three persons on board was en route from Portland, Oregon, to San Francisco, California. An extensive air search failed to locate the wreck. On 10/1/67 a deer hunter found N9388A and the bones of two occupants. Also found was a diary written by sixteen-year-old Carla Corbus that indicated she had survived in the wreckage at least until 5/4/67 and probably for several days longer. In fact Carla's mother and stepfather also survived for a lengthy period following the crash. Alvin Oien Sr., the pilot, attempted to hike out for help, but died presumably of exposure before reaching the nearest road. Mr. Oien's remains were found by hunters in 1968. The wreck is unmarked and buried at the site. This accident provided the impetus for the Federal Aviation Administration to enact legislation requiring all aircraft operating more than twenty-five miles from base to be equipped with an Emergency Locator Transmitter (ELT). These devices have proved to be effective in saving lives in subsequent searches.

3/15/67. *Cessna 182 N3999D* crashed in bad weather west of the town of Maxwell in Colusa County, killing all on board. Status of wreck today is unknown.

4/1/67. *Cessna 120 N2705N* crashed at 3,500' level near town of Covelo in Mendocino County. Wreck is marked and visible.

4/9/67. *Cessna* crashed in heavy woods SE of Clear Lake in Lake County. No other data available.

5/31/67. *Beechcraft Bonanza N3225D* crashed near town of Tennant in Siskiyou County. All three persons died in this weather-related crash.

6/18/67. *Piper J-2 N20112* crashed near Lake Berryessa in Yolo County, killing one person and seriously injuring another. Cause of this accident is listed as pilot error. Status of wreck is unknown.

7/1/67. *Piper Commanche N5716P* crashed south of Cecilville in Trinity County, killing both people on board. Pilot error was listed as the primary cause in this crash. Wreck is removed.

10/2/67. *Beechcraft Bonanza N5665K* crashed in bad weather near town of Callahan in Siskiyou County. All three persons on board were killed. Wreck is mostly removed.

1/18/69. *Aero Commander N8431C* crashed in bad weather near town of Gottville in Siskiyou County. Pilot died in crash. Wreck is in mountains west of Interstate 5 and north of Gottville. Status of wreck today is not known.

2/20/69. *Beechcraft 14 N6570N* crashed east of Highway 101 near town of Hopland close to Leech Lake Mountain. No other data available.

1/9/70. *Piper Cherokee 180 N7960W* crashed NW of Shasta Lake in bad weather, killing all three people on board. Status of wreck is unknown.

1/23/70. *Ryan Navion N91479* crashed near town of Guinda in Yolo County. Accident occurred in bad weather, killing all on board. Wreck is burned, upside down, and visible.

1/31/70. *Cessna 150J N51144* crashed while participating in Civil Air Patrol search mission in bad weather. Wreck was located 2/2/70 in mountains near town of Platina. Both the CAP pilot and his observer died in the crash.

5/3/70. *Convair T-29 USAF* crashed in cloudy weather near Hamilton Air Force Base in Marin County. Aircraft struck hills near base, killing thirteen and seriously injuring one person. Wreck is removed.

4/29/71. *Lightplane* (twin-engine) crashed in bad weather on Cahito Peak, north of Ukiah, killing one person. Status of wreck is not known.

5/28/71. *Piper Cherokee N9220J* crashed in mountainous country 20 miles SW of Red Bluff. All four persons on board survived with only minor injuries. Wreck is removed.

6/20/71. *Lightplane* crashed in Trinity Alps of southern Trinity County, killing two persons and seriously injuring another. No other data available.

11/11/71. *Piper PA-28* disappeared on this date in northwestern California. Wreck was discovered on 4/9/73 with the remains of both occupants still on board.

11/23/71. *Cessna 175 N7055M* crashed in bad weather seven miles north of Willits in Mendocino County. All four persons on board died in the crash. Status of wreck today is unknown.

1/1/72. *Beechcraft Bonanza N7333B* is reported at 39° 05'N and 122° 19'W.

Date unknown. *Cessna 120 N2238* is reported scattered and unmarked at 39° 26'N and 122° 47'W.

3/2/72. *Cessna 210* listed as unmarked at 39° 40'N and 123° 28'W.

4/22/72. *Piper Cherokee N5171S* crashed in bad weather east of Clear Lake, killing all four persons on board. Wreck is removed.

5/2/72. *Cessna 210* crashed in mountains NW of Willits, killing all on board. Wreck is scattered and visible.

11/26/72. *General Dynamics F-106 USAF Air Defense Command fighter* hit ridge three miles north of Hamilton Air Force Base in cloudy weather. Pilot died in crash. Wreck is removed.

12/72. *Lightplane N97366* crashed in heavy forest west of Clear Lake in bad weather. All on board died in crash. No other data available.

2/12/73. *Piper Cherokee N3055R* crashed at 3,200' level east of Clear Lake in Lake County. All on board died in this weather-related accident. Wreck is removed.

4/21/73. *Piper PA-28 N5171S* crashed in mountains near Ukiah. No other data available.

12/12/73. *Cessna 172 N35578* crashed in bad weather in the Trinity Alps, killing all on board. Wreck is scattered and visible.

1/13/74. *Piper Navajo* crashed in hills of Marin County north of Novato. Both persons on board died in the crash. Wreck is removed.

8/74. *Grumman F7F* crashed north of Yreka near Oregon border while on fire-fighting mission. Aircraft hit a tree and crashed, killing the pilot. Wreck is mostly removed.

10/27/74. *Cessna 150 N1487Q* crashed and burned five miles north of Vallejo in Solano County. All on board died in this weather-related accident. Wreck is partly removed and scattered.

12/22/75 *Rockwell International T-39D US Navy* crashed in stormy weather near Ukiah. Both crewmen perished in crash. Wreck is removed.

10/19/77. *Piper PA-28R* crashed in mountains two miles south of Calistoga in Napa County. Accident occurred in bad weather, killing both people on board.

11/5/77. *Cessna 172 N7330G* is listed as unmarked at 39° 24'N and 123° 28'W.

1/29/78. *Cessna 150* hit Mt. Burdell in Marin County in bad weather, killing both people on board. Wreck is removed.

2/12/78. *Lightplane* crashed in bad weather in mountains west of Vacaville, killing the pilot. Wreck is removed.

5/22/79. *Piper single-engine* disappeared in bad weather with four people on board. Wreck was not found until 9/25/79. Crash site is in Desolation Gulch near Yreka. Wreck is marked but hard to see.

2/13/80. *Lightplane N6788A* is listed as marked and visible at 40° 52'N and 123° 56'W.

Date unknown. *Cessna 172* is wrecked in mountains west of Winters.

2/13/82. *Piper (twin-engine)* crashed in bad weather four miles south of town of Sonoma in Sonoma County. Pilot died in crash and wreck is removed.

6/18/82. *Lightplane* crashed and burned in cloudy weather 80 miles west of Yreka in Siskiyou County. Four persons died in this accident. Status of wreck is not known.

7/2/82. *Beechcraft Bonanza N23725* crashed in Trinity Alps north of Weaverville in bad weather. Two persons perished in this crash. Wreck is to be removed.

10/24/82. *Lightplane* hit hills north of Vallejo in Napa County, killing all four people on board. Weather was a factor in this accident. Wreck is removed.

Date unknown. *Cessna 414* is listed in mountains west of Vacaville. Wreck is unmarked.

3/16/83. *Cessna 206 N1456M* crashed in mountains NW of Sausalito and was removed.

3/20/83. *Piper PA-28 N41576* is listed at 41° 14'N and 122° 46'W.

8/5/83. *Cessna 152 N7571T* crashed and burned at 40° 52'N and 123° 17'W.

5/2/84. *Piper Aztec* crashed in cloudy weather five miles SW of Ukiah in Mendocino County. All three persons on board were killed. Wreck is removed.

9/16/87. *Fairchild C-119* crashed while on fire-fighting mission six miles west of Castle Crags State Park in Shasta County. Three men died in this crash. Wreck is to be removed.

10/7/87. *Grumman S-2* of the State Division of Forestry crashed while on fire-fighting mission near town of Weft in Humbolt County. The pilot was killed in the crash. Wreck is in Klamath National Forest and is not yet removed.

12/15/87. *Piper Lance* crashed in bad weather near Ukiah, killing the pilot. Wreck is in mountains and is mostly removed.

4/2/88. *Lightplane* crashed in hills shortly after taking off from town of Calpella in Mendocino County. The pilot died in this bad weather-related accident.

3/8/89. *BD-4* is wrecked and unmarked at 39° 49'N and 123° 52'W.

5/24/89. *Piper PA-28 N4527F* is reported at 40° 18'N and 123° 32'W.

3/21/91. *Piper PA-28 N2776M* in mountains NW of Vacaville. Status unknown.

6/11/91. *Cessna 182 N3046Y* is listed at 40° 26'N and 124° 01'W.

10/2/93. *Cessna 177* crashed into hillside in bad weather, killing all four on board. Accident is near Petaluma, and wreck is removed.

7/12/94. *Aerospatiale HH-65 Dolphin USCG* crashed in heavy fog, killing all four crewmen. This helicopter was lost while searching for a missing fishing boat. Wreck is located on steep cliff near Shelter Cove in Humbolt County.

Date unknown. *Cessna 320 N3024R* is listed as unmarked at 40° 10'N and 124° 10'W.

The author with landing gear assembly from #42-7180 at San Miguel Island. (P. J. Macha) Region 9.

Date Unknown. USAF AT-6D. (B.F. Giebeler) Region 6.

1940-41. North American O-47. (D. Hammer) Region 5.

3/8/66. Cessna 182B. (M.J. Macha) Region 6.

2/14/76. Bellanca 230. (Willard Farhquar) Region 6.

3/19/66. PT-17. (NTSB) Region 4.

Resource Directory

United States Air Force
Historical Research Center/HD
Maxwell Air Force Base, AL 36112-6678

United States Navy
Naval Aviation History Branch
Building 157-1
Washington Navy Yard
Washington, D.C. 20374-5059

National Transportation Safety Board
Washington, D.C. 90594

Air & Space Smithsonian, published bi-monthly by the
Smithsonian Institution
900 Jefferson Drive
Washington, D.C. 90560

Air Classics, published monthly by
Challenger Publications, Inc.
7950 Deering Ave.
Canoga Park, CA 91304

Air Crash Investigation of General Aviation Aircraft by Glenn Ellis published by Glenndale Books

Wreckchasing by Nicholas A. Veronico, published by
Pacific Aero Press
P.O. Box 20092 Castro Valley CA 94546-8092

California Hiking 1995-96 Edition by Tom Stienstra/Michael Hodgson published by Foghorn Press

Wreck Finder Productions
222 6th Street
Seal Beach, Ca 90740
(714) 846 9213

ORGANIZATIONS AND ASSOCIATIONS
INVOLVED WITH AVIATION HISTORY AND AIRCRAFT ARCHAEOLOGY

AMERICAN AVIATION HISTORICAL SOCIETY
2333 Otis Street
Santa Ana, CA 92704
(714)549-4818

CURTISS-WRIGHT HISTORICAL ASSOCIATION/PROJECT TOMAHAWK
P.O. Box 9031
Torrance, CA 90508
(310) 325-6155

PROJECT TOMAHAWK is a non-profit corporation dedicated to the goal of restoring a Curtiss P-40B Tomahawk. The airplane under restoration is the only surviving American airplane involved in the Japanese attack on Pearl Harbor, *USAAF # 41-13297*. The plane was at Wheeler Field during the attack, possibly in a hanger. It was lost on a training mission in January, 1942, and was recovered by project members in 1985. Project Tomahawk needs members, donors, skilled aircraft workers, designers, parts, and especially financial support. If you would like to become a member, please send your tax deductible contribution to the above listed address. You will receive your Project Tomahawk membership patch and quarterly newsletter.

TIGHAR
2812 Fawkes Drive
Wilmington, DEL 19808
(302) 944-4410

UNITED STATES AIR FORCE AUXILLARY
CIVIL AIR PATROL
HEADQUARTERS—CALIFORNIA WING
P.O. Box 9117
Ontario, CA 91762-9117

Project Tomahawk

Project Tomahawk is a non-profit corporation dedicated to the goal of restoring a Curtiss P-40B Tomahawk. The airplane under restoration is the only surviving American airplane involved in the Japanese attack on Pearl Harbor, *USAAF # 41-13297*. The plane was at Wheeler Field during the attack, possibly in a hanger. It was lost on a training mission in January, 1942, and was recovered by project members in 1985. Project Tomahawk needs members, donors, skilled aircraft workers, designers, parts, and especially financial support. If you would like to become a member, please send your tax deductible contribution to: *Curtiss-Wright Historical Association, Project Tomahawk, PO Box 9031, Torrance, CA. 90508*. You will receive your Project Tomahawk membership patch and quarterly newsletter.

Historical Aircraft Crash Site Report Form

Please use this form to document crashes

Location

1. State:____________________________
2. Country:____________________________
3. Nearest City:____________________________

   Zip-Code:____________
4. USGS Quad:______________________7.5' 15' Photo Revised____________
5. Township:________________________

   Range:________1/4of______1/4of______1/4of______1/4of______
6. Coordinates:________________Lattitude:__________Longitude:__________
7. Descriptive Location: ____________________________
8. Landowner(s)(and/or Tenants) and Address: ____________________
9. Remarks: ____________________________

Crash Site Information

10. Nearest water (type, distance and direction):____________________
11. Site Vegetation:____________________________
12. Vegetation near site:____________________________
13. Site soil and Geology:____________________________
14. Soil and geology near site:____________________________

15. LANDFORM:____

____

16. SLOPE IN DEGREES:__________°

17. EXPOSURE TO THE ELEMENTS:____

____

18. CRASH SITE AREA:__________ YARDSX__________ YARDS__________YARDS²

19. METHOD OF MEASUREMENT: ____

20. DEPTH:__________

21. METHOD OF MEASUREMENT:____

22. DAMAGE TO PROPERTY, TREES, FENCES, ETC.:____

____

23. MARKED SITE: YES NO

24. HUMAN REMAINS:____

25. SITE INTEGRITY (DISTURBANCES/VANDALISM): ____

____

____

____

26. Site description: ____

____

____

____

____

____

____

____

____

AIRCRAFT INFORMATION

27. SERIAL #:______________________

28. AIRCRAFT #:______________________

29. SQUADRON #:______________________

30. OTHER #S: ______________________

31. AIRCRAFT MANUFACTURER: ______________________

32. MODEL:______________________

33. BRANCH OF SERVICE OR CIVILIAN:______________________

34. OTHER AIRCRAFT AT SITE (#?):______FILL OUT ADDITIONAL FORMS FOR EACH

35. # OF ENGINES: ______________________

36. TYPE: ____

37. SERIAL #S OF ENGINES: ____

38. TYPE OF LANDING GEAR: ____

39. Cargo/ordnance:____________________

40. Aircraft damage (fire, explosion etc.): ____________________

41. Salvageable parts:____________________

42. Date report compiled:____________________

43. Report compiled by:____________________

44. Address/phone:____________________

Sketch Map of Crash Site